Bitter Legacy

PICASSO'S DISPUTED MILLIONS

BITTER LEGACY

Picasso's

DISPUTED MILLIONS

Gerald McKnight

BANTAM PRESS

LONDON · NEW YORK · TORONTO · SYDNEY · AUCKLAND

TRANSWORLD PUBLISHERS LTD
61–63 Uxbridge Road, London W5 5SA

TRANSWORLD PUBLISHERS (AUSTRALIA) PTY LTD
15–23 Helles Avenue, Moorebank, NSW 2170

TRANSWORLD PUBLISHERS (NZ) LTD
Cnr Moselle and Waipareira Aves,
Henderson, Auckland

Published 1987 by Bantam Press,
a division of Transworld Publishers Ltd
Copyright © Gerald McKnight 1987

British Library Cataloguing in Publication Data
McKnight, Gerald
    Bitter legacy: Picasso's disputed millions.
    1. Picasso, Pablo – Estate   2. Inheritance
    and succession – France
    I. Title
    344.4065'2   [LAW]

ISBN 0-593-01034-5

Photoset by Rowland Phototypesetting Ltd
Bury St Edmunds, Suffolk
Printed in Great Britain by
Biddles Ltd, Guildford and King's Lynn

To Emma, Ben, Jack, and the unborn

ACKNOWLEDGEMENTS

I wish to thank and acknowledge all who kindly and generously helped in my researches for this book. I have omitted those who do not wish to be named.

In the family Picasso: Paloma, Marina, Maya and Emilienne.

Also Françoise Gilot Salk

Elsewhere: Jacques Perry, Christopher Jardin, Isabel Vacca, James Tomlins, Danielle Giraudy, Henri Cauquil, Sam White, Georges Berlioz, Dr Florence Rance, Stewart Newcombe, Nicolas Polverino, Dominique Bozo, Deborah Trustman, Sara Lavner, George Aczel, Robert Lewin, Jan Krugier and Nadine, David Duncan, and Paul Rossitter.

And in the work of preparation: Ann Kritzinger, Catherine Stylios, Mimi Wise, Lynn Curtis, Liz Dodge, Jeffrey Blythe and my friends Rayne Kruger, Denis Thomas, Donald and Nancy Newlove and Tim Warren.

CONTENTS

LIST OF ILLUSTRATIONS

Between pages 82 and 83

Entry to the Château de Vauvenargues.
Picasso's burial place: the Château de Vauvenargues.
Picasso's villa at Mougins.
Self-portrait of Picasso painted in Barcelona, 1986.
Picasso aged fifteen, 1896.
Picasso and his first wife, Olga Koklova.
Portrait of Olga by Picasso, 1917.
Paulo Picasso with his father.
Paulo with Claude and Paloma Picasso.
Paulo as 'Harlequin' by Picasso, 1924.
Paulo Picasso's funeral in Paris, 1976.
Emilienne Picasso, 1985.
Pablito Picasso with his grandfather.
Pablito in hospital after his suicide attempt.
Pablito's funeral.
The drawing room of La Californie, Picasso's villa in Cannes.
Marina with her children Flore and Gaël, 1985.
Maya Widmaier, 1985.
Bernard Picasso with his mother, Christine.
Picasso with baby Claude and Françoise, 1948.
Claude posing beside one of his own drawings, 1953.
Claude with his first wife, Sara, 1970.
Claude with Sydney, his second wife.

FOREWORD

In the spring of 1978 six heirs of Pablo Ruiz Picasso, perhaps the most versatile and prolific artist since Leonardo da Vinci and certainly the richest, inherited his fortune. The legacy was officially valued, after death duties, at £175 million. The inheritors were Picasso's widow, Jacqueline, his two legitimate living grandchildren, Marina and Bernard, and his three illegitimate *enfants adulterins* – Maya by one mistress, Marie-Thérèse Walter, and Claude and Paloma by a subsequent mistress, Françoise Gilot Salk.

The shock of Picasso's death on 8 April 1973 was not only felt by his family – it sent out more waves than the radio mast in the RKO Films trademark – but for his kith and kin it left an extraordinary situation. Picasso had made no will. He had amassed a fortune as immense as any artist in his own lifetime but left not a single direction, other than a few previously made gifts, as to its disposition. Whether he did so deliberately or not is the question which has intrigued the world ever since. Doubts about what he really intended have persisted throughout long years of legal embroilments, of family bickering and wrangling, and of valuation and counter-valuation of the enormous fortune in paintings, sculptures, drawings, ceramics, properties and hard cash left in dispute.

Picasso was a complex man. He died as he lived, a mystery. But now that the last brush stroke has been laid on the crowded, chaotic picture of his succession, the disputed millions apportioned and distributed, the extraordinary and damaging secrets of his bitter legacy can be revealed.

Five years ago I began my quest to unearth the background to the settlement of his fortune, hoping to document the experiences of the six who ultimately inherited. It was difficult to get anywhere near them. The Picasso clans – it is wrong to call them a 'family', as they are divided and always have been – have never sought publicity. Their unwritten rule is to keep as far as possible out of sight and communication with the world and with each other. Jacqueline, the widow, is so remote from the world that my letters and every entreaty failed to gain the slightest response. Fortunately, I was able to reach almost all the others – with the single exception of Bernard, the youngest grandson, who was only fourteen when his grandfather died – although in every case it required Maigret-like sleuthing to do so.

Picasso was not a conventional father or family man. In his lifetime he had cherished his children, both legitimate and illegitimate, while they were young, then refused to have anything to do with them when they grew up. Some of his most famous works document the depth of his compassion for the downtrodden, for the victims of war, the sickened and destitute. His interest in the bullfight can be construed as a humane analysis of man's basic barbarity. Above all he was supremely aware of mortal destiny and yet he took no account of the terrible legacy of confusion and despair which would result from his dying intestate.

He was fully aware of what he was doing, or failing to do. Indeed, the problems which would inevitably surround the disposition of his millions were predicted by him. To his favourite lawyer, the great Maître Roland Dumas (later Foreign Minister of France), he confided: 'Whatever madness you visualize [will follow my death], the reality will be worse.'

In the era of short-lived superlatives, it is nevertheless true to say that Pablo Ruiz Picasso is the supreme artist of his and our century; the breadth and brilliance of his *œuvre*, preserved in museums and private collections, eloquently attest this. But what of Picasso the father, the lover, the family man? The story of his disputed millions is fascinating in itself; doubly so for the new light it throws on the dark, labyrinthine recesses behind the artist's public face.

Bitter Legacy
PICASSO'S DISPUTED MILLIONS

1

STILL LIFE

Pablo Picasso's death on 8 April 1973 passed largely unnoticed in the southern French hill village of Mougins where
he had lived for the past twelve years with his second wife,
Jacqueline. The inhabitants of that part of Provence are
inclined to be blasé about the lives, even the deaths, of its
many celebrated residents; to treat them and their doings
with the same Gallic insouciance as is shown towards
the hot sun of the region and the daily consumption of
well-cooked food and simple wine. In addition, the Picassos'
insistence on privacy, 'from prying eyes' as Jacqueline put
it, had deeply upset the locals. Henri Cauquil, who has
lived in Mougins all his life, remembers the fuss it caused
when Picasso tried to erect a high wall round his already
isolated home, so as to prevent visitors to one of Mougin's
most valued monuments (a chapel erected by the Guinness
family on a hill overlooking the Picasso home) peering down
on him. In Cauquil's words: 'It would have ruined the
panoramic view from the chapel grounds, and not unnaturally there was strong opposition, so that in the end the
authorities refused to let Picasso build it. In its place he put

3

up a six-foot fence, which is almost as bad. It caused a lot
of ill-feeling.'

If one peers over the fence it is just possible to see part
of the long, low house where Picasso died, the rest being
hidden by the trunks and branches of tall cypresses. Mas
Notre-Dame-de-Vie is certainly remote, with only rough
dirt roads leading to its padlocked iron gates, threaded with
barbed wire and warning notices of 'Danger – savage dogs'.
The house has sixteen rooms, a vast studio and a cave-like
lower-ground-floor area in which the sculptures were
housed. Picasso was particularly fond of some of the sculptures but even more so of two almost worthless plaster
copies of Michelangelo's *Slave* which he discovered in the
basement of the museum in Antibes which houses many of
his works. 'They let me take them home,' he explained to
a friend in delight. 'Of course, I had to give them a whole
heap of my work in exchange.' The Mas is typical of houses
built for the better-off Provençals before the tourists arrived.
An ancient olive tree shades the front porch. A low 'cool-in-
summer' veranda runs the full length of the first floor.
Nearly three hundred feet above sea level the house seems
to sleep amid a forest of tall trees.

In his last years, Picasso turned inwards. Ill-health and
a failing interest in everyone but those he chose, by an
accepted *droit de seigneur*, to see from time to time – his
photographer friend David Douglas Duncan, and others
who lived nearby – made him a recluse to everyone else.
Jacqueline protected him with the doting care of a govern-
ess. She had followed his desire for simplicity in furnishing
the house. Its inside has a faded, comfortable look, unmis-
takably Provençal and unspoilt. Picasso had bought it after
their marriage in 1961 in his fury at the construction of a
block of flats near his great mansion of a home behind
Cannes, the villa La Californie, when an obsession with
uninterrupted views and personal privacy was already con-
suming him.

He had always moved a lot from house to house, room

4

to room. As he changed course in his work – moving through the tormented early 'blue', and the 'rose' period of his poverty and political commitment (he was a lifelong member of the Communist Party), to espouse surrealism, the world of the abstract, and finally ceramics and sculpture – so he also sought change in his companions, loves and habitats. Mas Notre-Dame-de-Vie was his last major acquisition. Not that he ever willingly dispossessed himself of the others. The studio in Paris, the seventeenth-century château at Boisgeloup in Normandy, the beautiful tenanted La Californie in Cannes, his chilly castle at Vauvenargues near Aix-les-Bains – all were kept waiting for him, under lock and key. In some of his former homes works of his were still lying where he had abandoned them, unprotected and subject to damage from mice, dust or damp. He boasted, perhaps truthfully, that he knew where every one of them lay, could always put his hand on a particular work if he chose to. If, as was discovered after his death, some were by then in a state of appalling disrepair, that was how he wanted things.

At the Mas he spent most of his time in the living room. Long and low, its walls and woodwork painted off-white and lit by double doors and windows, it retained the atmosphere of an earlier era, but the recently installed radiators kept him warmer here, he would say, than the rooms of his far grander castle, Vauvenargues, in which he had not spent any length of time for seven years or more. The Mas, with its views of forests and hills and the roofs of Mougins below, soothed and sheltered him. He made the room a jumble, but an idiosyncratic jumble; nothing was commonplace. Showing a friend the paintings he was working on one day, Picasso uncovered a study of a distorted white female figure with tiny, squeezed breasts and legs splayed open to thrust forward her elongated, distended sex. The woman had her arms spread wide in welcome, her face eaten on one side as if by some terrible disease. 'There are few girls like that any more,' he told his guest with diabolic humour. For him, impotent since the removal of his prostate gland in 1966, the fact was sadly academic.

The paintings lay about the room, leaning against chairs and tables. Picasso despised easels. He worked customarily above canvases laid flat on the floor. He painted where and whenever he wished to do so, always and infinitely. When an exhibition of his work drew artists in Paris to see it, he stayed at home painting. 'See how they waste their time when I can be finishing another work,' he said. The pale living-room curtains were seldom drawn. Picasso had chosen the hilltop Mas not only for its remoteness but also for the ever present light. It filled the room, streaming through the old french windows, flooding on to the large brocade-covered couch. A little-used television stood in one corner; occasionally, on winter evenings, he would watch the wrestling on it. His chair was the focal point of the room, a white swivel model with a black cushion and a sheepskin spread across its back which he would wrap around his legs or shoulders if he grew cold while working. There was no special place for this. He worked or amused himself wherever he sat, using the chair (which he called his 'throne', and reputedly had had for fifty years) as an all-purpose platform. Here he read letters delivered to the remote house by a postman on a motorcycle, or his daily copy of *Nice-Matin*. Sipping a brand of herb tea called 'Queen of Fields', he would work on etchings and engravings, or simply chat with the occasional visitors allowed the privilege of an audience.

After his death Jacqueline is said to have preserved the Mas air of comfortable simplicity. Five hundred yards above the house, on the hillside, Picasso built a pergola with square stone pillars and iron trelliswork. She spends a lot of time there in summer, reading or listening to the music she loves. For her, Picasso's spirit is as much alive as ever in the old stone house.

April 8 dawned a chilly spring day, and the light flurry of snow that fell later was unusual in that mild region. In the streets and squares of the old Roman town, fitful sunshine sparkled on snow-rimed surfaces. All that winter there had been gossip about Picasso's failing health. Some said he had been unable to shake off the bout of pneumonia which had struck him before Christmas, but few believed the old lion was actually in the last throes of his incredibly long and lusty life. There were some, however, who knew better.

Nicholas Polverino, proprietor of the popular little Le Fournil restaurant, heard dire reports from his aunt, Inez Sassier. He was not unduly concerned. Since the feud about the wall, Picasso was not a popular figure locally. 'We had no contact with them up there,' Polverino explains. 'We knew Jacqueline and saw her in town from time to time, always very dignified. But nobody really went near the place except their friends, who would drive up from Cannes and Vallauris and places of that sort.'

Like almost everyone else in Mougins, the restaurant proprietor could hardly have cared less about what went on in the shuttered guarded confines of Picasso's retreat, but his Aunt Inez nursed warm memories of its reclusive inhabitant. She had spent years living with Picasso and his family. She lives close to her nephew, in a pretty apartment overlooking the valley. In her living room, looking at the array of framed photographs of herself with the Picassos, Inez still remembers her first encounter with the great man who, some say, was later her lover and even offered her marriage. 'I don't talk about those things,' she says, but her eyes tell their own tale. She and her older sister, Sabartez, were teenagers, two attractive Spanish working girls, when Picasso first came to Mougins. He came in customary style, accompanied by the voluptuous Dora Maar, his Yugoslav companion of the late thirties. With world war threatening, Picasso was bent on enjoying an abandoned spree, a vacation which was to extend intermittently over three years, 1936 to 1938.

Mougins was the discovery of Picasso's great friend, the poet Paul Eluard, and his wife Nusch. The story goes that

7

Picasso had had a mild affair with Nusch, but such was the bond between them that it had not affected his friendship with Paul. It is hardly surprising that he managed to delight in Mougins. Not only was Dora Maar there but also fifteen-year-old Inez and her seventeen-year-old sister. Inez, it seems, was working for a *parfumier*, picking jasmine blooms which were then crushed to provide the floral essence, nowadays all too often derived from chemicals. After the holiday meeting, she and her sister were taken to Paris by Picasso. He employed them in his apartment in the rue la Boëtie with Inez as chambermaid and Sabartez as cook. When Inez later married, Pablo let the couple take over a small flat adjacent to his new studio in the rue des Grands Augustins. Inez thereafter acted as the painter's occasional caretaker as well as remaining a close friend.

Inez has vivid memories of those early holiday visits to Mougins. Picasso first put up at the Hôtel Vaste Horizon, facing on to the Boulevard Courteline in the lower reaches of the town. It is a Spanish-style two-storey building of wide arches and verandas. It is said (though nobody knows the truth of the story) that, in the large suite which he occupied, Picasso painted one entire wall as high as the beamed ceiling with a mural of fauns and maidens in an erotic dance to Pan. Whether this was objected to by less full-blooded guests or was simply decorated over, it no longer exists. The present management takes understandable pride in the legend.

Inez prefers not to talk in detail about those days. She keeps to herself her feelings when she first heard of Picasso's fatal illness and death. Like many others she had found it difficult, if not impossible, to reach her old companion once Jacqueline, the strictest of nurses, cocooned him from the world. For almost a month a discreet local doctor, Florenz Rance, had attended him. Picasso's own doctor, a man he trusted despite his acutely suspicious nature, was too sick (he subsequently died) to look after him. Rance found himself paying almost daily visits to the recluse in the Mas where Jacqueline fluttered round him like a trapped moth. 'She cared for him as no man has ever been cared for before,' the doctor says. 'Obviously at his age, ninety-one, he had to be spared any emotion. His heart was weak and she had to obey his every whim. She called him "Monseigneur", you know. "My lord"! I don't want to give intimate details, but it was not easy for her.'

Nor was it easy for the doctor. 'A responsibility, rather like looking after the King of France! I wasn't too scared but I was a little worried. Professionally speaking, that is. To tell the truth, I was relieved when he died.' He has nothing but admiration for Jacqueline. 'The poor woman lived through a very sad time. She had lost her god. She felt attacked on all sides. After his death there were regiments of lawyers, experts, bailiffs, coming and cataloguing everything. The longer it lasted, the more money they earned. You have to understand, everyone was getting a finger in the pie. I can tell you she, Jacqueline, was sickened by what they did.'

Nevertheless, she knew her duty. Jacqueline Roque had met Picasso in 1952 at the start of his ceramics period. She had come to work for relatives in the Vallauris Gallery where he operated. Divorced, and with a young daughter, Catherine, she befriended Picasso during the stormy ending of his long affair with Françoise Gilot, the most important mistress of his life. Six years after Olga, his estranged wife, died, Picasso married Jacqueline. Whether she believed it necessary to free him from his past, or whether she simply felt that a man of his age, possessed of his magnificent gifts, should be protected from all intrusion, Jacqueline thereafter placed an impenetrable barrier between him and much of the outside world. Since this pointedly excluded his ex-mistresses – not only Françoise Gilot and her two children by Picasso, Claude and Paloma, but also his earlier lover, the ever adoring Marie-Thérèse Walter, and her daughter by him, Maya – difficulties were bound to arise. After his death, these flared into open conflict.

9

Dr Rance became aware of the bad blood flowing between the widow, who had been childless during her life with Picasso, and the earlier remnants and offspring of Picasso's polygamous past. 'There was obvious friction,' the retired doctor explains. 'You can't imagine how sad it was for Jacqueline. As if my wife had died and then all the children arrived saying "I want this!" and "I want that!" There were packing cases piled high with his works. And she had been forbidden by him to sort all that out while he was alive.' His sympathy is heartfelt. 'Remember, there was forty-five years' difference in age between them, and she had got him at the worst time of his life, when he was ageing and becoming dictatorial. He was nice to me, very nice, but a little bossy. I mean, he lived exactly as he chose to the very last. Sleeping most of the day and staying up most of the night. She was *devoted* to him. But to be his wife in all this was far from easy. For instance, he would call up and say he was coming home with twelve or fifteen friends. And she had to give them food! To him everything was always possible, he never saw obstacles. No wonder she called him "Monseigneur".'

Writer Patrick O'Brian believes there was no thought in Picasso's mind of imminent death. 'He was working again in the early spring,' O'Brian's biography records, 'getting up at about noon and sometimes staying on in his studio until six the next morning.' The day before he died, Picasso had invited friends to dinner. 'But when he went to bed that night,' O'Brian says, 'he had a feeling of breathlessness, and the local doctor detected a bad infection of his lungs and the strong likelihood of very serious heart-trouble.' So the dinner party had to be cancelled. Dr Rance confirms this. 'He had to be spared any worry. Everything had to run smoothly, which was difficult in the circumstances.' Even at this point, the doctor says, Picasso was being harassed by family friction. 'You have to understand that *everyone* was interested in his going . . . it is really terrible the way people are.'

And Jacqueline, it seems, was handling it all in her own, highly selective way. Picasso's one legitimate child, his son Paul (Paulo) by his first marriage to Olga Koklova, was in Paris. He alone received reports of his father. Picasso's illegitimate children (Maya by Marie-Thérèse; Claude and Paloma by Françoise) had been barred from their father's presence for years. There was little or no communication with them except through lawyers. Least welcome of all at the Mas was Paulo's family by his first wife, Emilienne Lotte, who lived nearby in Golfe-Juan with their two grown-up children, Pablo (Pablito) and Marina. Paulo's second wife, Christine Pauplin, was with him and their teenage son, Bernard, in Paris. None of Picasso's grandchildren saw much of him, and the entire family seems to have lived in a state of frustrated awe of the eccentric old man and his guardian wife.

Much of the friction the doctor noticed sprang from a succession of lawsuits, wrangles and claims which the family – in particular Françoise's two children, and the poverty-pleading Emilienne and her children – inflicted on Picasso. Picasso was a tough old Spaniard with the obstinacy of a fighting bull in a corner, but age and illness had weakened him. Latterly he had withdrawn into himself, leaving Jacqueline to play the part of the dragon in the cave-mouth. It was she who had to fend off all approaches from these outsiders.

And finally the enormous reserves of brute strength, which had allowed him to carve stone or stand painting for hour upon hour, failed. According to Dr Rance, nothing but sheer over-use, the ageing of too many organs, killed him. 'Heart and lungs were giving out simultaneously,' the doctor explains. O'Brian says Jacqueline saw it coming. The day before his death she called in 'an eminent cardiologist, a friend of Picasso'. Apparently the specialist flew from Paris, taking the early-morning plane. 'He saw at once that there was no hope, but he did what he could to make his patient comfortable. Picasso was fascinated by his instruments, full of liveliest curiosity. He got up and shaved – he wanted to show the specialist some of his pictures in his studio. But presently shortness of breath made him lie down again.'

More recently Jacqueline has painted a different picture. 'When the doctor came in the morning, I wanted to get up,' she told someone last year. At the time, apparently, she was lying beside Picasso, warming him with her body. 'Pablo held my hand and said, "Doctor, are you a bachelor?" The doctor replied that he was. Picasso said, "You're wrong, it's good to have a wife."' O'Brian's less charitable version is that 'he sank gradually through the morning, but with no pain; and in a lucid moment towards the very end he spoke quite clearly to the specialist, a bachelor, saying, as he reached out his hand to Jacqueline, "You are wrong not to marry. *It's useful.*"'

Whichever version is true, it seems certain that it was almost noon, nearly time for the old clock in Mougins to strike the cracked chimes of *midi*, and that Picasso was trying to rise from his bed when a last spasm took his breath away for ever. The artist who had despaired of God because 'he has no style', the man who had told his writer friend Jean-Paul Crespelle that 'death is the only woman who never leaves me', was dead.

Jacqueline, according to Dr Rance, could hardly believe it. Her fanatical devotion was more than love, closer to obsession. In those first hours she seemed unable to accept or measure the full extent of her loss. At a practical level she was still in command – issuing notices, summoning functionaries, attending to formalities – but she must have known, even then, that his passing left a void in her life that would never be filled. A large part of her had died with him. While her husband was alive everything had been done for his health and comfort in order to keep the irritating intrusions of the outside world to a minimum. Now, all at once, the obligations of that world were pressing in on her and her guiding spirit was gone. She alone stood guard over his treasure trove, the mountain of great art which lay in her protection, here and in his other houses and studios. She had helped him with the photographing of many of these works, listing and keeping some sort of record of where they all were. To be left in possession of such a vast, scattered collection, to bear the responsibility for it all, would have been an overwhelming prospect for an expert in the field. Jacqueline's grounding in art was at best limited.

In addition, she knew and feared what might happen as a result of her husband's irresponsible past. There were others who would contest this inheritance, who would demand a share of it. She had had experience of them, and of their anxiously pressed claims. These 'others', the issue of his rakish early life, had been denied recognition in his lifetime. She felt it her duty to ensure they did not receive credence and riches now by getting their hands on Picasso's riches. Françoise Gilot Salk was the woman she had most to fear from, the mistress Picasso had lived with for ten years before Jacqueline had come into his life. It was Françoise who had mothered two of Picasso's illegitimate children, Claude and Paloma; Françoise who had persuaded their father to support them during their education, despite their parents' acrimonious parting; it was his former mistress who had instigated long legal battles for her children's right to share in Picasso's estate after his death, and who even now was pressing these claims – still unsettled – from her new home in America.

While he lived, Jacqueline had been able to protect him from these interlopers. After his death, she must be doubly on her guard. Ten years previously Françoise had played into her hands, by writing a book, *Life with Picasso*, which Jacqueline denounced as a scandalous invasion of his privacy. The book had put paid to Françoise's children's visits to their father, which had previously been regular holiday events in summer and winter. Shortly before the book's publication, Claude and Paloma were refused access to their father. Jacqueline saw to it, on Picasso's orders. Henceforth, he was to be left to get on with his life and his phenomenally demanding work without interruption from his troublesome offspring. He must never be invaded by tiresome people of any sort. She knew how Françoise felt about the children's expulsion. Now that Picasso was dead, the mistress who had preceded her in his life, who had borne the children Jacqueline had been unable to give him, was plainly a threat. Fortunately, Jacqueline could depend on Picasso's trusted and eminent lawyer, the great Maître Roland Dumas (later to become France's Foreign Secretary under his friend, President Mitterrand), to support her against these claimants. He was the first person to be notified of Picasso's death, and was by her side while she deliberated on her next move.

On Jacqueline's desk, facing the screen of split cane hung with postcards and pictures of Picasso's works, was the cream-coloured telephone by which the news of Picasso's death would reach the world. She picked it up. There were calls to make which could be put off no longer. Paulo, Picasso's only legitimate child, his son and surely his heir, was summoned. He came hotfoot from Paris where his life until then had been a shabby succession of drinking bouts and emotional crises. The story that he had acquired bad habits, including that of drug taking, from Jean Cocteau as a small boy has never been denied. In his daughter Marina's recollection he was nearly always drunk, or partially so. Marina blamed the way Picasso brought up Paulo for the breakdown of his marriage to her mother.

The three of them – the distraught widow, the lawyer who might have modelled his grave, discreet behaviour on Charles Dickens's Mr Tulkinghorn, and the wayward son – made a bizarre cabal in the silent house where Picasso's body lay awaiting their disposal. Dumas, the *éminence grise*, knew what had to be done. He was fully and expertly aware of the rights and position of everyone concerned in what was to become, in legal eyes, *l'affaire Picasso*. He knew of the new Act, which had passed into French law in January of the previous year, 1972, which gave equal rights of succession to illegitimate children – *enfants adulterins* – who successfully proved their parentage. He also knew that the Act made it incumbent on such claimants to register their claim *in the two years following their twenty-first birthday*. The provisions of the new Act were most directly applicable to Claude and Paloma, whose mother, Françoise Gilot Salk, had always been vociferous in pressing their claims on Picasso. But Claude was already twenty-five and his sister twenty-three. Time might be against them. Maya, the other 'adulterous' daughter of Picasso's earlier mistress, Marie-Thérèse Walter, was older still. If the Act was strictly interpreted, any claim from these three could be forestalled.

Dumas assured Jacqueline and Paulo that they – the widow and the son – were the only true heirs. Under Napoleonic law, children in France take precedence in succeeding to a parent's estate, though certain provision is made for a widow as next of kin. A portion of the estate may be set aside for bequests and gifts made during the deceased's lifetime, but in this case there seemed, in Dumas' eyes, to be no other rightful beneficiaries. Jacqueline, he advised, must do nothing to encourage the outsiders in the family to entertain false hopes. Paulo's children, by both his marriages, were equally to be dissuaded from any hopes of getting anything while he was alive. Picasso had not wanted to provide for them or he would have done so expressly.

There was no will. Of that vital fact the lawyer was absolutely sure. He had shared his client's confidence, knowing and understanding Picasso's abhorrence and fear of discussions about death, especially his own. 'My father had refused absolutely to leave a testament in his lifetime,' Paulo was to explain later. 'He told me he couldn't bear to mention such matters, which is very Spanish. He said it is believed to hasten one's own death to make a will.' So there was nothing to guide the three of them except the statutory powers allotted in France to the widow and legitimate children. Any claims by the outsiders could be rejected and repulsed. The little river running round the guarded boundaries of Mas Notre-Dame-de-Vie was to become a moat, a metaphorical rampart raised against all the dubious claimants.

Paulo would deal with his own children, Pablito and Marina, and their mother, Emilienne. He would also handle his wife, Christine, and their schoolboy son, Bernard. He would tell them the truth, that only he and Jacqueline were to inherit his father's fortune. As to Maya, now married to a marine officer, Pierre Widmaier, and living in Toulon with their children, she would be told, by the lawyer if necessary, that any claim she thought she had would not be recognized. The same would most certainly go for Françoise Gilot's children: Claude, who was working in America as a photographer, and Paloma, who had a job in Paris, designing jewellery. They, too, must be disabused of any misplaced expectations.

Jacqueline had only the haziest notion of the extent of the fortune in paintings, sculptures, pottery, engravings, property and hard cash which her husband had left, but she knew it must be immense. There were not only the paintings he had kept and refused to sell, but also many others he had disposed of only to buy back at a later date. The representative collection of his own works, 'Picasso's Picassos', was a priceless record of every stage in the master's evolution. There was besides the 'secret room'. In that locked chamber, to which Picasso alone had the key, he had preserved the works, some forty in all, of famous contemporaries who had given him valuable canvases out of friendship and regard for him. He had left clear instructions on what he wanted done with those magnificent paintings. They were to be given in his name to the country's greatest artistic treasure house, the Louvre. It was his belief that all great art was intrinsically universal, that it should not belong to any one man. Thus these works had been 'his' only during his lifetime on extended loan. As the work of primarily French artists, they belonged to France and must revert to her on his death.

An appalling task faced Jacqueline: every item of the estate must be catalogued and valued. Before anything could be settled, the scale of the inheritance must be gauged and its security urgently ensured. Immediate orders were given to the effect that every work of art must be carefully crated, then taken in guarded vans at night to bank vaults from which they might be removed with the full authority of Maître Dumas and herself.

Equally pressing was the need to make the funeral arrangements. Where and how was Picasso to be buried? His political allegiance and avowed lack of any practising religion ruled out a church or cathedral ceremony. Anything grand – a funeral with official honours and tributes – would have been anathema to him. He had craved privacy, grown tired of the claims of the inquisitive world. In death also he must remain out of range of the common herd. How was it to be managed? How could Picasso's interment be carried out in secrecy when so many people would expect to be invited? Some would no doubt take it as a mortal insult to be excluded. And there were important celebrities, famous painters among them, who would feel they had a perfect right to attend.

Jacqueline's dilemma was obvious. To bury him there in Mougins would be to attract unseemly attention. There would be no way to keep out the family, the media, or even the nosy villagers. Though the Mas was isolated, and the barbed-wire gates guarded day and night by men Picasso had picked (as well as Afghan hounds, kept to frighten off trespassers), it was still far too public. So where? Bois-geloup in faraway Normandy? The seventeenth-century château bought by Picasso in the twenties and left deserted by him for nearly forty years was too remote. La Californie perhaps? No, the baroque fifteen-room villa in Cannes was currently tenanted by Picasso's Spanish secretary, and was besides not nearly secluded enough. Vauvenargues, then.

The fairy-tale château had been bought by Picasso in 1958. Perched on its own mountain near Aix-les-Bains in South Central France, it was protected by 2,600 acres of impenetrable wooded grounds. It seemed the perfect place. No matter that Picasso had felt chilled by the house, or that he found the lack of plumbing and heating, its air of pervasive gloom, so lowering to his spirits that he had not visited it for years, and had almost never worked there. Vauvenargues ideally suited Jacqueline's requirements. His grave would be more inaccessible there than in any other available site.

Once her mind was made up, Jacqueline moved quickly. Picasso's body was taken away privately with none of the family, other than Paulo, knowing or being informed of its destination. Those who, like Claude and Paloma, knew the phone number of the Mas sent expressions of sympathy and such support as they felt able to offer. With relations as strained as they were, these cannot have been excessive. The telephone was now in constant use. Jacqueline had to arrange for gravediggers, undertakers, all the usual details of a private funeral. A priest was recruited, and two members of the local Communist Party. The latter were invited to honour what she felt would have been Picasso's wishes, and anyway showed a nice sense of theological balance. For a headstone she decided to use one of Picasso's sculptures. It was taken to Vauvenargues where preparations for the burial were already under way. In her haste and grief Jacqueline was not to know that the sculpture, an angelic female figure, had been modelled (according to Maya) upon Marie-Thérèse, Maya's mother, an early mistress of Picasso with whom he had never fully broken off relations.

The irony of his widow's putting the effigy of an adoring mistress over his grave would certainly not have been lost on Picasso. Paul Diegue Joseph François de Paule Ruiz Picasso was no respecter of convention, still less of women's feelings. To him, as he openly said more than once, all women were 'either goddesses or doormats'. In Jacqueline, the companion of his latter years, he had found the most

luxurious of doormats, but left to herself the doormat became an avenging angel. She barred all outsiders, including
members of Picasso's family, from his last rites. Jacqueline
did far more than carry out what she believed to be his last
wishes. In barring his children and grandchildren from the
obsequies, she was in effect declaring open war. The battle
for the rights of these illegitimate children and legitimate
grandchildren, a bitter struggle which was to rage for five
years and cost three lives, had begun.

The only known photograph of the funeral (taken by an
intrepid photographer from *Paris-Match* magazine who must
have crawled up the steep hill through dense pinewoods,
somehow avoiding dog, bodyguard and barbed wire, to get
it) shows the grave only a few yards from the foot of the
stone steps leading up to the old portico of the château, a
little to one side of the forecourt. The burial site is a shaded
spot, perhaps one that Picasso had painted. The diggers
had had to work hard to cut through the frozen earth but
had managed it in good time. Jacqueline had insisted that
the funeral should take place on Wednesday, 16 April, only
eight days after Picasso's death.

By then the weather had turned almost bitter. A flurry
of early-morning snow lay on the gravel driveway and
coated the fresh earth turned by the gravediggers' spades.
It was a strange gathering that assembled around the
home-made graveside. A group of fifteen figures, no doubt
encompassing servants and gravediggers, can be seen in the
photograph. The family was represented by Paulo (drunk,
according to Marina), Jacqueline and her daughter. Of the
six who would eventually inherit the vast fortune left by the
world's wealthiest artist, only one was there to pay their
last respects to the man who would make them multi-
millionaires.

The others had pleaded to be allowed this last moment
of contact with their departed parent or grandparent, but
Jacqueline had refused. When Pablito and Marina begged
their father, Paulo, to intercede on their behalf, he agreed

only to meet them in a café in Vallauris. They were not allowed to go to the house. There, Marina says, Paulo 'turned up drunk, and told us we would inherit nothing, and that it was out of the question for us to come to the funeral, or to see our grandfather's body, since Jacqueline would not permit it'.

Jacqueline may have been, probably was, unaware of Paulo's brusque and callous dismissal of his own children. It is understandable that she felt impelled to carry out her dead husband's wishes, as she imagined and interpreted them to be. She may, it is charitable to suppose, have had no knowledge of the agony of those outside the locked gates, barred from the simple ceremony in the old castle grounds at Vauvenargues. Perhaps she did not know not only that Marina and Pablito, who lived nearby, were being refused entry at the very gates of their grandfather's home but also that Maya, Picasso's daughter by Marie-Thérèse, and her half-brother and half-sister, Claude and Paloma, had come likewise to pay their respects and had been turned away. This much she was aware of: she knew that young Pablito, who had a menial job in the local post office because his grandfather would spare not one sou more for his mother's upkeep than the pittance awarded her under a court order at the time of her divorce from Paulo, had already, less than a year before, tried forcibly to gain entry to his grandfather's house to see him. Jacqueline knew because she herself had had him ejected, her servants physically barring his way and throwing his motorcycle into the moat-like ditch of Mas Notre-Dame-de-Vie. She had even called the police to have him removed, and allowed the dogs to be let loose to scare him on his way.

During the last ten years of Picasso's life, Jacqueline had steadfastly refused to allow any of the outsiders into his domain. Now that he was no more she had a double duty to honour his memory and to protect his wealth. In doing so, she had the strong arm and wisdom of Maître Dumas to support her, as he had so often supported Picasso against the encroachments of his undeserving offspring. Dumas would keep them at bay for her. Dumas was her strength against all of them: against Françoise Gilot Salk in America, scheming to gain places in the succession for her children, Claude and Paloma Picasso; against Marie-Thérèse and her daughter, Maya; and against the children of Emilienne, Paulo's ex-wife, whom Picasso had detested and had wanted nothing to do with. Pablo had more than once said to Dumas, during their conferences together over the incessant court actions which Claude and the others had forced on their father: 'Naughty little children should stay out of sight.' Jacqueline would see to it that they did.

2

PABLITO'S MESSAGE

Tragically, one of the 'naughty children', Pablito Picasso, was incapable of accepting any such dismissal. He went home from the meeting with his drunken father to the unpretentious little villa in Golfe-Juan where he and his sister lived with their divorced mother, Emilienne. Paulo's rejection, his conveying of Jacqueline's refusal to allow the grandchildren to attend the funeral, overwhelmed his son. As Marina says: 'Pablito, my brother, could not bear to hear his father say that to him. The next morning he drank poison.' After a sleepless night Pablito found a bottle of concentrated bleach, used for cleaning lavatories and drains. In a fit of uncontrollable despair he drank a litre of the corrosive fluid. It acted as quickly as lime. By the time he reached the hospital it was impossible to save his digestive organs. Pablito had sentenced himself to die in the most horrible way imaginable – by slow starvation.

Had he but known it, he had everything to gain by staying alive. In his twenty-four years he had risen only as far as becoming a lowly assistant at the local post office and yet in one respect he had been blessed. He was, by all accounts, a remarkably good-looking young man with Picasso's dark, penetrating eyes under attractively straight brows. In photographs lovingly preserved by his sister and mother in their respective homes he is shown to have had film-star features. His dark curly hair is set off by a well-trimmed beard; the neat suit and patterned silk tie worn for the photo session give an almost aristocratic air.

Yet this young man with everything to live for succumbed to a sudden, terrible impulse to destroy himself as publicly and lingeringly as possible. If he had resisted it, Pablito would have lived to inherit one of the largest portions of his grandfather's estate. Today he would be a multi-millionaire. He could not, of course, at the time of his suicide, foresee how close he was to this; his own father was bluntly telling him that he and his sister would 'get nothing'. Nevertheless, it is hard to understand the savage intensity of Pablito's act. In his immature, somewhat unstable, mind he must have believed that nothing less than the horror of this appalling death would touch his father, melt Paulo's hardened heart towards his ex-wife and daughter. It is just possible that Pablito did not really mean to die, believing that the gesture would be enough and that medical aid would reach him in time to prevent fatal damage.

Even his family are mystified. They can only assume that his suicide was an expression of lifelong resentment, and perhaps envy, of his famous grandfather. This had been exacerbated by Picasso's hostility towards Emilienne after her divorce from Paulo. The limited financial means provided her, the constant poison of living in close proximity to one of the wealthiest and most celebrated men in the world without enjoying even the crumbs from his table may well have brought the essentially simple young man to an unbearable pitch of frustration and fury. If he had used his body as an advertisement, dousing himself with petrol and making a flaming torch of himself outside the locked gates, his death could not have made a more shocking statement. That, above all, must have been what Pablito intended.

He and his sister had had a good education, the funds for which had been provided by Paulo, as required by law, but had originated from Picasso, who had grudgingly underwritten them. Pablito's only epitaph must be that, while he had been equipped to understand the nuances of the great world his grandfather moved in, he lacked the fortitude to cope with his own exclusion from it. His grandfather had so much – wealth, fame, universal respect – and during his life had given him so little. Even after death, it seemed the pattern remained unchanged. Pablito, excluded and rejected still, made a last spectacular protest against the indifference and neglect he felt he had been shown in his life. 'He never really was raised with my father or anything like that,' his aunt Paloma explains. 'That and the fact that he had the same name was plainly not a help. He was *called* Pablo Picasso. He had to live with this. I think it just proved too much. For us it was different, it is our life. For Pablito, it was sort of unreal.'

Pablito's sense of unreality stemmed from a boyish idealism, a belief that his mother, sister and he himself deserved far more from their wealthy and illustrious namesake than the maintenance provided under court order, amounting despite their appeals only to some seventy pounds a month. 'We lived in misery,' Emilienne, his mother, told reporters at Pablito's bedside during the weeks leading up to his death. It was as if she had at last found a focus in her son's tragic death for her own bitterness against her ex-husband and his famous father. The hospital, De la Fontonne in Antibes, where Pablito was taken, became the centre for a spate of ugly publicity. The horror of Picasso's grandson's slow death attracted world interest. Not surprisingly, the more popular press showed scant regard for the feelings of the family. Huge pictures of Pablito's wasted frame appeared, swathed in bandages and with tubes clipped to it. His harrowing words were quoted in glaring headlines: 'I wish to join my grandfather.'

When finally, on 11 July, Pablito died, having lost half his weight, he was extolled in a two-page spread in *Franche Dimanche* as 'the poor man' whose death and the reason for it were to be luridly divulged by his mother: 'For the first time his mother reveals the terrible truth'. According to this newspaper report, Pablito died as a result of 'crippling poverty' in which Emilienne and her family had been forced to live while 'arch-millionaire' Picasso had all the riches he could command. 'If I had had money,' Emilienne cried, 'my son might still be alive today.' It was as far as Emilienne, or the newspaper, felt able to go. But the inference was obvious. In the mother's eyes, Pablo Picasso and his son were responsible for Pablito's sacrifice.

On the day after her son died, Emilienne told French reporter Yvonne Gugielmo that lack of money had prevented her providing treatment which might have saved his life. 'A fortnight ago, when he took a sudden turn for the worse,' she said, 'the doctors at Antibes, Drs Bonnet and Sauvan, wanted to have him moved to the Rothschild Hospital in Paris in a special air ambulance. Unfortunately, I have to live by public charity, and the Social Security formalities which could have provided funds for the bus took too long. When the authorization came through it was too late. My child was dead.' She then went into harrowing details of her lack of money and its dire consequences. Emilienne knew, of course, that her revelation that Paulo Picasso, son of the world's richest artist, had allowed his son to die for lack of funds would scandalize the French public, but she had endured Picasso's obloquy, the failure of her marriage to Paulo and the difficulties of living on limited means. Now, her only son was lying dead from his own impetuous and terrible act. Why should she pull her punches? 'Three months ago he was a good-looking young man, full of life,' she told reporters tearfully. 'When he died he didn't even weigh thirty kilos. I would have liked to bring specialists to his bedside, but I couldn't afford it. I didn't have a penny. I couldn't even afford a night nurse for Pablito!'

Emilienne praised the Antibes doctors and the hospital for doing all they could. She focused all her bitterness on the poverty that had restricted her ability to do more to help him. 'All his life he had wished for two books, encyclopaedias, which I had never been able to buy him,' she sobbed. 'Then, when he was dying, three of his friends clubbed together to buy them and I brought them to him. He hadn't the strength to turn the pages. He couldn't even swallow a drop of water. Nevertheless he tried to smile and comfort me. "Put them on the table in front of me," he whispered, "so that I can at least look at them."'

The afternoon before he died, Pablito had come near to collapse. She was told that he would be placed in intensive care for attempted resuscitation. A nurse, 'with tears in her eyes', told her that she had to leave. 'I'll never forget the look in Pablito's eyes,' Emilienne said. 'He stared at me with complete understanding. We were both crying. I said: "See you later, my darling." He gave a pathetic little smile and said: "Even in war, soldiers who die cry for their mummy."

'I implored them to leave me a little longer at his side, but things had to be done quickly. I waited in the corridor and saw him wheeled away. His face was deadly pale. I went outside into the hospital garden and sat on a bench, waiting for Marina to come as she always did in the early evening. When she arrived they told us to go home and not to worry as they were thinking of having Pablito transferred to Paris, anyway. It gave me renewed hope. Maybe all was not lost. And when I called up the hospital every hour until midnight the reports were no worse. Then at three a.m. the phone rang and Marina answered. I asked her: "Is the plane ready at last? Are they taking Pablito to Paris?" She told me: "He just died, Mummy." We wept in each other's arms for a long time.

Then I fetched from his cupboard his navy-blue suit, the only one he had, a white shirt and a blue tie. We drove back to the hospital in Marina's little Volkswagen. What shattered me, like a hot iron in my heart, was that my son had died alone.'

Later, she was told that Pablito's father had offered to pay for the funeral. 'He had ordered another coffin, more luxurious than the one we could afford. But what's the point?' she asked. 'It doesn't matter any more.' In the same mood of bitter recrimination against both Paulo and his late father, Marina, Emilienne's daughter, who was employed as a helper in a home for handicapped children, told an interviewer: 'My father had left us without any money at all for the previous three months. Every time we asked for help, we were brushed off with a refusal. It has always been the same. He has shown complete indifference to us. And we are his legitimate children! We bear the name of Picasso! It's a name even harder to carry now that it has cost the life of a twenty-four-year-old young man.'

Pablito's agonizing death would have caused even more concern among the various Picasso clans if the family had not been so deeply divided. In one sense it united all Picassos, legitimate, illegitimate, related by blood or by marriage, in a common feeling of horror, but it did little or nothing to untangle the roots of their basic problem: that as a family they were driven by jealous resentment of each other's position in Picasso's eyes.

During Pablito's parents' brief marriage, Paulo had been anything but an exemplary husband and father. They married, Emilienne for the second time, on 10 May 1950. Divorce followed little more than three years later. In that time the records suggest that the marriage veered between passionate love, in which two children were conceived, and mutual infidelity. At the time of the separation and divorce, social workers intimated that there had been several instances of adultery. There was also, in Paulo's case, a report of cruelty which, if it did not physically damage them, may well have scarred the children psychologically.

It is not known exactly when Paulo's serious alcoholism began, but it had certainly accompanied some of the worst passages of his life, of which this was one. His early record of persistent illness, including hepatitis, suggests that drugs and drink may have changed him from the shy loving son of Picasso, whom Françoise had known, to the weak and emotionally unstable man whose behaviour the social workers damningly documented. Emilienne was equally condemned, her way of life severely criticized. Her right to retain the children was allowed only on condition that a careful watch on their welfare be officially maintained.

The failure of the marriage and the precarious position in which it left Picasso's grandchildren beg the obvious question: why did he leave them to flounder in low water when he was among the world's most successful and wealthiest men? A single painting could have been sold for sufficient money to maintain them for the rest of their days. Then, again, why had Picasso allowed his weak son to stumble into such an unsuitable match? Paulo had grown up with no marked gifts or aptitudes. He had nothing of his father's creative fire or personality. The interest he had in motorcars resembled that of a small child in railway engines. It was an immaturity which gave Picasso, when he spared time to think of it, immense pain. It may well have been that the artist in Picasso recoiled from helping what he might have termed 'lame dogs' over stiles, even when the lame dog was his own son. His early poverty in Madrid and Paris had hardened his conviction that all who could should stand on their own two feet. When Paulo showed no aptitude for doing so, his father resigned himself to having a son who did nothing but tinker around with motorcars.

His inability to hold down any job led Paulo to ask his father for financial help. He was curtly told: 'If you can't find work, and you want to stay close to motorcars, you'd better become my chauffeur.' Odd as this may seem, the idea was not without merit. Paulo enjoyed driving the grand old relics of motorcars of his father's *équipe*, particularly the superb black Hispano-Suiza which Picasso treasured. Paulo the chauffeur and son soon became a notable figure in the Mediterranean towns of southern France, seen leaning against the door of Picasso's automobiles, waiting for his 'master'.

When Paulo met Emilienne, however, Picasso should have given more guidance than he did. The marriage was an obvious travesty. Despite the fact that its good patches led to a small and delightful family, a son named Pablo after his grandfather but nicknamed Pablito to differentiate him, and a daughter, Marina, the marriage was a source of furious dissension. When it collapsed, Picasso blamed Emilienne for what was equally his son's failure. Admittedly, Emilienne was impetuous and highly strung, but it was Paulo who lacked serious intent. If the judges at the divorce hearings found it hard to decide who, if either, was less worthy to safeguard the future of their children, there seems to have been no reason for Picasso to be so biased against his daughter-in-law. Emilienne's fighting spirit (she was a Protestant from Alsace) hindered any *rapprochement*. At one point in the various legal battles with her ex-husband, she demanded through her counsel a clinical report on Paulo's sanity. Rejecting this, the judges categorically stated that they had serious doubts about her own. They reduced her plea for an increase in maintenance by more than half.

What she took from the fractured marriage certainly did not compensate for what she lost. Picasso's unfeeling remoteness, Paulo's enmity, and her children's bitter incomprehension of the reason for their plight were nagging wounds which refuse, even today, to heal. Only now that Marina, her daughter, has received her share of the millions which Picasso never intended her to have can Emilienne enjoy the luxuries she was deprived of in Paulo's short lifetime. But the sense of loss she still feels today is irreparable. Pablito's childhood drawings, little more than scribbles, hang framed on the walls of her luxury villa in Cap d'Antibes. They and her tears attest to the love she bore him and the pain caused by his futile gesture and unnecessary death. All this, they seem to say, would have been his. The house is protected by electronically controlled gates, guard dogs and a living-in bodyguard, Daniel Van Tin, an ex-marine who, with his wife and son, takes more than ample care of her. She discourages visitors.

Otherwise Emilienne seems almost too determined to make up for lost time. She is still trim and in good physical shape, practising daily on gymnastic exercise equipment set up in a special room of the long house and swimming in the lovely freshwater pool set in the flower-decked lawn. She goes regularly to fitness classes in Juan-les-Pins. In her late sixties, this sadly distressed woman is not letting herself go, but any mention of Paulo's action in preventing her children from attending their grandfather's funeral, of the tragedies, including her son's suicide, which ensued, of the legal struggles which have bedevilled her daughter Marina reduce her to uncontrollable displays of emotion. While she talks, tears run down her small rouged cheeks. The air of coquetry which she seeks to preserve as a reminder of her youth sits awkwardly on such distress. There are passages in her life which she still does not like to remember.

The days that followed Picasso's burial were torment for her. She had already suffered greatly from her father-in-law's indifference. In his lifetime, Picasso had refused even visits from her. She was never allowed to feel, let alone behave as, a member of the family. Yet, whatever she had done, the legal decision given against Paulo would seem to indicate that he had behaved in worse fashion. According to newspaper reports (though, in consequence of the curious habit of France's lesser courts of destroying all but the barest 'extracts' of cases brought before them, these cannot be substantiated), Paulo was barred by court order from contact with his own children. The ban was to last for ten years. Certainly neither Pablito nor his sister Marina was under the slightest doubt as to which of their parents was the more guilty party. In their eyes their mother was grossly ill-treated. She was the victim of whatever cruelty may have led to the divorce. They stood beside and with her in attempts to provide for them at a level to which, as a Picasso, she felt entitled. They could do no more.

Paulo had his famous, powerful and wealthy father behind him. Emilienne was alone. Whatever else her ex-husband suffered from, it was not loneliness. With his famous surname he was always able to attract attention. Emilienne was less fortunate. For three years, until the age of twenty, she had suffered from acute tuberculosis of the spine. The after-effects of the disease are with her still, causing a weakness in her back which is the main reason for her frenzy of exercising activity. Yet Paulo saw fit to make life still more painful for the woman he married, and by whom he had his first young family.

Emilienne lives surrounded by photographs of the son she loved, whose death has scarred her life. There are consolations in the grandchildren her daughter has given her, but Pablito's death remains a central symbol of her suffering at the hands of not only Paulo but also his father. Her son's drawings emphasize this as nothing else. 'They were done when he was only three,' she explains. 'When Pablito realized who his grandfather was – the famous painter – he never dared to draw or paint again.' She ignores the fact that Pablito's rejection of his artistic inheritance coincided with her separation from his father. Perhaps that is understandable. By all accounts the trauma of those days when both his mother and his father were drinking, fighting and abusing each other openly left scars that never healed in both the children. Paulo's behaviour after his son's death clearly shows the depth of his wounds and the bitterness of his vengeful feelings.

Emilienne was photographed at Pablito's graveside, supported by her daughter and Paloma. Paulo's absence, though noted, was rather remarkably not commented on by the several attendant journalists in their reports on the funeral. It was also strangely reticent of the press that, although some twenty photographers were reputedly present, few pictures appeared and these were not given anything like the coverage which the shots of Pablito's wasted body had received. In the long weeks before he died, Pablito more than once begged his father's permission to be buried alongside his grandmother, the Russian dancer Olga Koklova, in the family vault in Vallauris provided for her by Picasso. Paulo refused, as he also refused to meet the costs of his son's hospital treatment, which ultimately had to be paid for by a charity.

Entreaties by a distraught Emilienne utterly failed to move her ex-husband. Paulo's wounded feelings over the broken marriage were plainly still so painful that he could stoop to taking this revenge on his child, even while he was dying the most agonizing death. The one gesture Paulo allowed himself to make was to meet the cost of Pablito's funeral in the Protestant cemetery at Antibes. This could hardly be called generous. He stood, at the time, to inherit half his father's entire fortune. As a final insult he stayed away from the ceremony itself. One wonders what can have prompted such an omission. One also wonders how much Picasso was to blame for having imbued his son with such a cruel streak. It was left to the ubiquitous Maître Dumas to soften the blow. 'I am profoundly affected, as are all those who knew him, by the tragic end of young Pablito,' the lawyer declared after the funeral. 'But to put an end to erroneous rumours and speculation concerning the attitude of my celebrated client towards him [Pablito] I must point out the truth. Picasso in his lifetime assumed full responsibility for the boarding-school education of both Pablito and Marina at the Chateaubriand Institute in Cannes, right up to the end of their studies. He and his wife wanted no publicity for this. But I must today, and only today, make it known in order to correct what is being said.'

Dumas went on to shed the first and only ray of public light on one of the most mysterious aspects of the whole *affaire Picasso*. He allowed himself to give, with Jacqueline's approval, the only explanation so far vouchsafed for certain members of the family having been banned from Picasso's funeral. Maître Dumas explained that the ban stemmed from 'a serious incident involving young Pablito with law enforcement authorities in August 1972', in other words, some eight months before Picasso died. What happened on that day, 17 August 1972, had previously been known to only a few people. In the lawyer's carefully chosen words Pablito tried to force an entry to the locked sanctuary of his father and stepmother in Mougins. He had apparently just been told by his father that if he did not like his job at the Post Office 'there were jobs available for street sweepers'. Tormented by the contrast between his family's lack of means and his grandfather's wealth, he decided to break into the forbidden grounds. Picasso's men sent for the police and set the dogs on the intruder. In reply to pressing questions by newspaper reporters, Maître Dumas also revealed that Pablito had carried a poster, or banner, with him. 'It declared his intention of staying in the grounds until his grandfather agreed to see him.' According to the lawyer's statement, the incident ended when Pablito was 'finally persuaded to go away'. The use of savage dogs and armed *gendarmes* was indeed persuasive.

Apparently Picasso had seen the attempted invasion of his privacy as a personal threat. Henceforth, no member of the family would be permitted to disturb his peace of mind. He and Jacqueline gave strict instructions to that effect as Claude and the others found when they, too, tried to enter the barred walls of Mas Notre-Dame-de-Vie. Jacqueline had extended the ban to include his funeral. But what had caused a great artist with avowedly humanitarian ideals to

34

impose such an inhuman sanction on members of his own family? Perhaps the explanation may be deduced from a closer examination of the tortuous recesses of Picasso's psyche.

3

INFERNAL CLOWN

Picasso's secret was that his soul brushed the stars while his feet were in the gutter. Arthur Koestler declared that his character defied any simple analysis. 'Incompatibility of temperament would be too facile an explanation for the breakdown of their relationship,' Koestler wrote in his review of Françoise Gilot's book, *Life with Picasso*, in 1965. 'He had lived with a variety of women with a variety of temperaments and the outcome had been much the same. The incompatibility was not between the characters but between the temperament of genius and the institution of monogamy. God knows, it is a brittle affair even for ordinary mortals; in the case of geniuses of the Picasso type, it reduces itself to absurdity.'

In some ways, too, absurdity was a keynote to the man himself. Picasso liked to play the clown, to attract attention by practical, often harmful, joking at the expense of others. His refusal to leave a will, or any specific instructions as to the disposition of his vast wealth, may well have been impelled by this wicked love of leg-pull. In his famous statement to Dumas, so often quoted and repeated by him

37

in his lifetime, that 'far worse will follow my death than has ever been seen in my life', there is more than a hint that he secretly enjoyed the thought of the squabbling to come.

On 19 April 1973, ten days after Picasso's death and three days after his sadly private funeral, while the red earth of Vauvenargues was still fresh on his grave, Maître Dumas made an interesting announcement about his famous client. 'Pablo Picasso, in his great wisdom, knew that there would be much contention, much avidity, after his death. Yet he adopted an attitude of complete serenity and calmness, declaring that he had decided to leave the whole affair to justice and the law. All those who are making claims at the present time, who think they have something due from him, should take note of that. . . .' Dumas, like Jacqueline, plainly believed that Picasso had intended to let the law decide how his fabulous wealth should be divided. He deliberately rejected any means by which he could have shown love and generosity to the children he said he loved. A multi-millionaire, what would it have cost him to have left clear indications as to his wishes – a signpost for Jacqueline and others who had to select and distribute the valuable pieces? He did nothing of the kind.

Among his jokes were some that could never be lightly passed over. Paloma, his daughter, remembers his being 'perverse in a child-like sense'. She told Joan Juliet Buck of *Vogue*: 'He knew the value of what he did.' The value, and the hurt it could cause. One day, before she and her brother were forbidden entry to their father's house, she had seen the black joker at his most capricious. Art-historian Douglas Cooper paid them a visit. One side of Cooper's car, a black Citroën, had recently been damaged. A large panel was painted over with red anti-rust paint. Picasso was immediately enchanted. 'Wonderful! I'll draw on it!' he declared. Paloma says he picked up some children's chalks and 'started doing sublime drawings all over the red patches'. Before Cooper's eyes, his car was transformed into a magnificent original Picasso worth a small fortune. When it was done, Picasso suggested they should go to the beach for a swim and Cooper set out gingerly behind Picasso's car in his now priceless vehicle, worrying all the time that the chalk would blow away.

Paloma says: 'It was an entirely deliberate joke by my father. He liked nothing better than humiliating art experts and dealers.' As Cooper drew up at the beach, he jumped out to inspect his car. An appreciable amount of the drawings remained. Picasso, Paloma says, 'took a discreet look' and decided the joke had not gone far enough. There was still too much of his work left intact. Innocently, he announced: 'Why here? It's much better in St-Tropez. Let's go there.' Once again the wretched Cooper was forced to drive off. Picasso, in his chauffeur-driven car, led the way. The road was dusty and the wind strong. Cooper tried to reduce speed, but Picasso wasn't having any of that. 'Full speed ahead!' he ordered his driver while beckoning the historian from the rear window to keep up. Paloma told Buck: 'By the time we got there, poor Douglas was in a state of complete shock. There was nothing left of the drawings on his car.' And Picasso, she says, was delighted. If any evidence is needed to confirm the likelihood that fear and dislike of the mention of death, particularly his own, were not the sole reasons why Picasso left no will, this example of gratuitous mischief provides it.

'You can call it a caprice if you like,' Paloma's mother says. 'To be so full of death that you don't want to think about what must happen to those who follow you is a kind of caprice in its own way. But I actually believe [his action in not leaving a will] was a concatenation of many things.' Ruthlessness, certainly, was one of them. Françoise will never be able to rid herself of the memory of his words when she left him, taking their children. For more than ten years she had been his mistress, his companion in everything he did including painting. Her own work had been conducted parallel to his. She was leaving Jacqueline already installed in her place. 'I shall never see you or the children again,'

Picasso told her brutally. To Françoise the cold sincerity of his dismissal carried the force of a revelation. She could see as never before the strength and ruthlessness of his character. 'We were suddenly the opposite of all that we had been to him while we were with him. Instead of white, we were all black. At that moment I learned that for Picasso there was no in between.'

For a long time in her self-imposed exile, Françoise, a student of psychology, pondered the often conflicting traits in the man she had for so long adored. For herself the callousness of his rejection was bearable, but for her children to be barred from their father's presence by his spiteful desire to hurt her seemed terrible. It was Picasso, she explains, who had wanted and persuaded her to have them. She had agreed, largely to please him. And on her own terms. She had told him at the time: 'I am satisfied with things as they are, because I'm completely free and so are you. If you want us to have children together then you must make the same commitment as I. You must never turn against them. Your duty to them will be the same as mine, with no difference between us.' Picasso's acceptance of this was also clear in her memory. 'He told me "Of course! What do you mean? What do you think I am?" et cetera. "As long as you are there, everything will be theirs."'

She saw nothing sinister in this qualification until after Jacqueline had replaced her, and she and the children were in Paris. 'It was a sort of blackmail situation which I had not foreseen at all, even as a possibility. I'd thought anything like that from Picasso would be too ridiculous, but that was how it turned out.' She felt betrayed then. 'Caught by my own innocence. He intended to use the children to tie me to him. I hadn't believed anybody would do a thing like that, but he did. It was like the worst kind of divorces, where the children are mercilessly used by parents as ammunition. I find that one of the most disgusting things in the world, yet Picasso used our children in just this way. It was absolutely barbaric.' The paradox was that

Jacqueline, as Françoise knew, could *not* bear Picasso's children. She had undergone operations to enable her to conceive, but these had failed. The fact that Françoise, the ex-mistress, had carried his children and was bringing them up was a bitter cross to bear.

After the split from him, the children became pawns in what Françoise calls 'a merciless state of war'. And she was ready for it. As well as studying art, at the time she met Picasso she had also received a grounding in legal economics. During his lifetime, it served her well. 'I told him he thought I was weak, because I was nice to him and tried to keep things on a positive basis between us. He was very wrong. I could give blows as well as take them. If he fought me, I would fight him.'

They finally compromised, she sending the children to him during their holidays and at some weekends. She was scrupulous in keeping her side of this arrangement. Equally, she was shrewdly ensuring his continuing interest and involvement with them by doing so. But one Sunday he shocked her. 'He called in the evening and told me flatly that he intended to take them away. I would never see them again, he said, unless I complied with some demand he was making. He was prepared to do that, to use the children as blackmail! It sickened me.' At the time, she was living on what she could make from her painting plus the small maintenance payments Picasso was providing under law while the children's education continued. 'I also had, fortunately, a small legacy from my grandmother, so I was independent.' But it was a struggle which would have overwhelmed a lesser woman.

Françoise believed, and went on believing until his death, that Picasso would eventually honour his undertaking to her about the children. 'He knew I would not have agreed to have them if he had not given me his assurance that they would be as much to him as they were to me. I couldn't believe he would cheat me or them over that.' When, towards the end of his life, he opposed their lawsuits seeking

41

their rights of succession, she felt cheated. 'I hadn't any proof of what he'd said. I thought what we had agreed was stronger than any legal paper. I was completely taken aback by what finally happened. If Picasso had done the worst possible thing you can think of to me, I would have found that acceptable. But what he did to the children was something I could never accept because it was contrary to everything he had promised me.' She had to face up to the knowledge that the man she had loved and given her life to for ten years was betraying his promise to her. 'I realized that power, his ability to dominate others, was his supreme interest. Once I was away out of his reach he had to crush me. He couldn't let me live. What was the ammunition he needed to do this, to destroy me utterly? My children, of course.'

Françoise had learned in law school that 'natural' children such as hers – adulterous in French law since Picasso had been married at the time of their birth – had few rights, let alone of succession. If and when she died, Claude and Paloma would lose everything. They would be thrown on the state, deprived of even the right of adoption by their grandparents and dependent on national assistance. The one way she could prevent this, Françoise discovered, was to make them wards of a trust, a *conseil de famille*. The idea had other advantages. 'I had invited Pablo to be one of the trustees, which meant that he was officially recognizing the children as being under his protection. Also I had put some of the money my grandmother left me on the head of each of my children and persuaded Picasso to provide maintenance as his share. So that was another useful evidence of his paternity.'

The trust became effective in 1955, the year in which Françoise married. The marriage to painter Luc Simon infuriated Picasso because, in law, her husband now shared in the children's trust. It delighted Françoise, who needed all the outside help she could get. 'Then, when the following year my daughter Aurelia was born, all hell broke loose!

That really did it!' An infuriated Picasso took the one action he believed would ruin Françoise once and for all. He instructed Kahnweiler, his main agent, to cancel the contract made during the time Picasso and Françoise were living together under which the agent had agreed to sell her pictures in his gallery. 'Kahnweiler told me he had to do as Pablo wanted. He couldn't afford not to. He could no longer take my work so that if it had not been for my grandmother's bequest I should have been penniless.'

It took Françoise a whole year to recover from this act of revenge. Meanwhile, Picasso's fury was seeking other outlets. He ransacked the home they had lived in, seizing all the pictures he had painted of her during their years together. It seemed he intended to destroy all records of their time together. He then transferred the focus of his anger on to the children themselves, who were hurt and astonished by his subsequent refusal to let them visit him. It showed that he felt he could trust nobody in his intimate family circle, not even Jacqueline, to look after his affairs. Boasting he would live for ever but knowing he must soon die, Picasso wanted his great volume of work, the collection he had so carefully gathered at the Mas and elsewhere, to be preserved intact. Jacqueline would, of course, have guarded it faithfully, and yet he never took the step of making her his heir.

Françoise believes that he left the muddle to solve itself, deliberately, spitefully, and for deep and curious reasons. 'He had sadistic tendencies,' she says. 'I believe he was what can truly be called a sado-masochist, because he also felt the hurt he inflicted on others. There were many times in our life together when he would make an aggressive move only to end up at my feet, begging for punishment. If I had any sadism in me I would have served him that dish and he would have loved it!' She believes it is this trait, more than any other, that explains his refusal to make a will. 'Pablo knew, as a very intelligent man, that he was doing something very destructive in his reluctance to settle matters, so that at least the heirs would be guided by his stated wishes. Only a desire to hurt can provide the missing piece of the puzzle. You see, it fits symmetrically with the anxiety and lack of confidence he had in himself.'

In her educated opinion the whole drama of his life resembles an antique tragedy, one in which Picasso the god held total control while his heirs and assigns did his bidding unconsciously. Yet he welcomed their dominion once they had earned it. 'You may think I am exaggerating, I am not. I don't know how to say it more clearly. Deep down, there was a lack of self-confidence in Pablo. It is very strange, because he never, never physically destroyed any of his work except in that one way. *That* was his act of self-destruction, of self-mutilation. It is very paradoxical – two polarities acting on one human psyche.' It led, so she believes, to his tendency to show himself as a clown. 'He liked those who were slightly against him to write him off in this way, saying "Oh, he's only a clown." The absence of the will therefore became a parody of the clown tumbling on to the stage in the full glare of the floodlights.' And not just a friendly, fun-providing clown. 'Oh no, there was an infernal machine in there. When I was with him I could see into it, see it working. In a way I felt privileged to have both seen it and escaped! After all, I am still here, and my children were not destroyed.' Eventually, she believes, the machine worked against its master. 'That was why I had so much tenderness and love for him,' she says. 'Because he was also so fragile. Ultimately, I can find only compassion for Pablo. He did it to himself.'

In her book about their shared life Françoise goes deeply into Picasso's complex psyche, revealing the artist as part caring lover, part monster. Recalling stories he had told her about his unending stream of sexual conquests, she wrote: '. . . he had a kind of Bluebeard complex. It made him want to cut off the heads of all the women he had collected in his little private museum.' As one of the most influential and intimately connected of this gallery, she was in a strong position to level this accusation, though Jacqueline was incensed by the book's more candid passages. 'He didn't cut the heads off entirely,' Françoise continued. 'He preferred to have life go on, and to have all those women who had shared his life . . . letting out little peeps and cries of joy or pain, and making gestures like disjointed dolls to prove there was life left in them.' A pointless exercise, as Françoise pointed out: 'It hung by a thread, and he held the other end of the thread.'

Yet he could be magnanimous in defeat. When she beat him in a legal battle over the book, at a time when they were speaking only through lawyers, Picasso astonishingly telephoned to congratulate her. 'Bravo!' he cried. 'You won!' Françoise, in spite of her surprise, remained coolly aware that this was the voice of only one aspect of Picasso's amalgam of contradictory attitudes. She remembered that he had always liked those who bested him in a fight. 'I'm delighted to please you,' she said with ill-concealed irony.

As a student she had studied the works of Carl Gustav Jung. She found that many of the events in Picasso's troubled family history fitted the Swiss psychologist's theories. The biggest shock was to discover how closely her own experience at Picasso's hands, particularly in regard to their children, fell into the semblance of classic Jungian case-history. A common theme ran through Picasso's relationships with women, she decided. They were nearly all neurotically dependent, in need of a father-figure. His selection of them seemed largely dictated by this quirk. 'When Pablo was choosing a woman, he looked for someone who was in a weak social position. That allowed him to do what he wanted with her,' Françoise says. There were exceptions, of course, including her own situation. 'But after his first affair with Fernande Olivier – who was already married, which was why she refused to have Picasso's child when he wanted her to, so he lacked the power to crush her as he crushed the others – the pattern became marked.'

By Françoise's reckoning, it was the subconsciously savage undercurrent in Picasso's domination of women that had caused the death of his next mistress, his beloved 'Eva', Marcelle Humbert. 'She is the second one we know anything about. And he *did* crush her. She did die. He took her away from another artist. And it's strange because, when I was only eighteen and didn't know Picasso, I met some of that artist's family and heard their side of the story.' Françoise was told that Picasso had wrenched his darling playmate out of a happy relationship with another man who wanted to marry her. 'That loss, coupled with her poor health, proved too much.'

She saw the same influence brought to bear on Picasso's earlier marriage to Olga Koklova. Françoise had suffered the embarrassment of the rejected Olga's lifelong harrying of Picasso. In her book she recounts how the cast-off wife, who would never allow Picasso to divorce her, followed them about. On a beach once, she came up unnoticed behind them and deliberately walked over Françoise's hands. 'Olga had a psychological problem, for sure. She was a woman from the minor Russian aristocracy who had been left with absolutely no-one. I believe her father had died during the revolution, her brother had been killed as an officer in the White Army.' Françoise saw their relationship as parallel to that in the Chaplin film, *Monsieur Verdoux*. 'Olga was the victim who would not be missed. She was entirely alone, with nobody to worry about her.' In picking out his wife when she was working with Diaghilev's *corps de ballet* Françoise believes that Picasso had deliberately chosen a mate who would depend utterly on him. 'She was only a second dancer, not a star. He knew she would have to rely on him for everything. She was therefore ideal.'

The same theme, she says, ran through most of his other choices of women. 'After that came Marie-Thérèse. Her family was always on the brink of disaster. Her careless mother had not even bothered to get married! There again, Pablo could do as he pleased. There was nobody looking after Marie-Thérèse's interests. Nobody to tell him to stop, to say "That's enough!"'

When he made Françoise his mistress and shared ten years of his life with her, she believes Picasso made the mistake of equating her with these dependent women of his past. 'He thought I was made of the same stuff. In fact, I was not quite the simple little student I appeared when we met. [This was in 1943 when Françoise was, in a friend's opinion, 'a twenty-one-year-old Florentine virgin'.] Someone from my social background would have understood this, but Pablo did not know it. He didn't see that I had travelled and spent a lot of time in England. All that interested him was that I was adrift from my family. That I'd left home, after terrible rows with my father – which made me seem like any other woman nobody cared about and who needed his protection.'

It was, as she says, 'a war situation. I believed at the time that life had little value. I was rebellious. Picasso entirely missed the point, the reason *why* I felt the way I did. Why I was always contemplating suicide and so on.' Intellectually, Françoise was going through a self-destructive phase, having walked out to escape her father's harsh discipline. At the time they met she seriously believed that her life, *all* life, was worthless: 'not worth a penny'. He mistook this typically adolescent despair for weakness, a need to escape. 'Whereas I had an architecture in my character which grew stronger all the time I was with him. In the end I became too challenging. When I started painting, successfully, and Kahnweiler gave me the contract, Pablo felt threatened. I was treading on his ground.' She, too, had made a mistake. She had shown that she could manage without him. 'In Picasso's eyes, once I had earned recognition in my own right as a painter, I had to be slain. I had become opposition, no longer a nobody to be crushed at will. I was a threat.'

His classification of women as 'goddesses or doormats' challenged Françoise's instinct for survival. She was neither. 'He *thought* I was. Because at that time I seemed susceptible, a really easygoing type. That was why he misjudged me so

47

badly. Once I had set myself up as a painter I was competing with him on his own level – I wasn't a doormat or a goddess any more!' Nevertheless, she played the part for him. 'Fortunately, I didn't need much sleep so I could be his goddess, day and night, whenever he wanted. In all the years I was with him, I never managed more than four hours' sleep a night!' Qualities such as these, and her ability to ride a horse well, earned his admiration. But they also threatened the relationship. 'He saw me as a kind of Joan of Arc. A woman who had to have the upper hand.'

In Picasso, she believes, the need for submissive women was paramount. Those who challenged too closely had to be thrown aside and destroyed. 'The most deadly element in our relationship was that I might have gained control. That could not be tolerated. In that role I had to be wiped out – it was a perfect reason for killing me. Paradoxically, if I was weak I also had to be exterminated. So there was no way I could remain with him.'

At first she had believed that if she stood up to him during his tantrums and displays of temperament she could be a help in his work. It was an illusion. He did not need a self-sufficient helper, he needed a doormat. 'In the end, the fact that I could run my own life and manage on my own was what drove the wedge between us.' And because Françoise was becoming more and more accepted by his close circle of friends: 'I was really a threat to him.' In their calmer moments, they discussed this. She told him: 'You of all people should be able to understand greatness and accept it in others. Nobody can put you in the shadows. So why not let them share a little of the sun?' She did not realize until after they had parted that for Picasso the idea of someone else sharing his God-given sunshine was anathema.

A perceptive writer, Calvin Tomkins, noted this quality in Picasso's paintings of Marie-Thérèse. In an article in the *New Yorker* on 30 June 1980, he remarked: 'It is as though Picasso, in his rage to encompass and depict the world

48

simultaneously from every angle, had possessed his beloved inside and out, body and soul. . . . One wonders how Marie-Thérèse survived it.' The sad fact is that their love affair did not. Picasso left her, returning only fitfully thereafter. Yet his paintings of her, Tomkins said, were 'lyrically erotic . . . she appears to be gazing placidly into the depths of her own voluptuous nature'. It was a voluptuousness which, in spite of everything, burned like an eternal flame for both of them.

Marie-Thérèse held the key to Picasso's closest secret. The blend of cruelty and compassion in him seems to have been understood subliminally by this simple, non-intellectual woman. The Picasso who left his succession to the winds of chance, to the wrangles, squabbles and lawsuits which followed his death, was no stranger to her. But in the family it is believed that Marie-Thérèse blamed her daughter for Picasso's loss, coming so soon after Maya's birth on 15 September 1935. Possibly, it is said, Picasso not only found Dora Maar's arms more enticing but also nursed a subconscious fear of all girl children which turned him against Maya.

This curious belief is based on a story vouched for by a woman who knows Picasso's intimate life story. It is linked to the death of Picasso's younger sister, Maria de la Concepcion, during his youth in Spain. While Maria lay ill her brother prayed daily for her recovery, vowing solemnly that if she was spared he would never paint again. When she died, Picasso felt betrayed. He had offered his greatest gift in return for her life, and God had declined to accept it. It is perhaps not too fanciful to detect a subsequent scarring of his psyche, a subconscious dread of the vulnerability of girl children. By christening their daughter Maria de la Concepcion (later shortened, at her request, to Maya) he and Marie-Thérèse were further commemorating this tragedy. Shortly afterwards they parted, and Marie-Thérèse was never able to reconcile her natural feelings for her child with the loss of the greatest love of her life. She could never forgive her child for it, and she and Maya grew apart.

A recent biographer further believes that Picasso 'often applied to his relationships with women the principle he pronounced one day when he was making a pottery dove: "You see, to make a dove you must first wring its neck. Women," he likewise declared, "are suffering machines."' Picasso, in his lifetime, did his best to make them so. Similarly the agonizing events of his succession, its settlement, and the toll it took on everyone involved made suffering inevitable.

Françoise Gilot was studying the philosophy of pain and pleasure, taking instruction from an Indian *swami*, when she first met Picasso. He was instantly fascinated by her pursuit. 'I had achieved a point where these categories did not touch me, but he wanted more. I soon realized that what Pablo wanted was both to suffer, and to make people suffer.' She recognized the same trait in his painting. 'He was always waiting for something to appear. Like the child who takes the clock to pieces to see what makes it tick, then cannot put it together again.'

At the beginning of their relationship, he asked if she was interested in the writings of de Sade. 'He was probably trying to shock me but I had read some of de Sade's work and was not particularly impressed. Also I prided myself on being an intellectual. I said "For me, these kind of stories are not very illuminating."' He obviously found them so. Furthermore, he put de Sade's theories of pleasure, heightened by inflicted pain, into practice. Françoise says: 'That explains a little of the relationship with Jacqueline. The executioner can also adore being the victim. And certainly I didn't want to play that game with him. I told him I was the slave of love, but not of him.' Her financial independence, and refusal to have a third child when he wanted her to, were her avenues of escape. 'He wanted to anchor me. He thought he had taken me out of my own class and that I could never return to it. A third child would keep me with him. But I told him jokingly, "Yes, I would like to have another child, but not with you!"'

It was after he had conducted a casual infidelity with Geneviève Laporte that Françoise decided to leave him. Immediately, Picasso began pressing her to have another child – a deliberate ruse, she saw, to keep her tied to him. 'You know, there's no greater unhappiness than to depend on somebody like Picasso for your needs. Because he is a sadist, he will apply the screw. That was why he wanted to have a further child. I saw his game, which is why I beat him at it.' Nobody had done that before. As Françoise recalls. 'You can't believe how terrible it was. His ego was so tremendous! And he suddenly had to realize that I was free to leave him! That was especially bad because I was very useful to him by then.'

The image of the minotaur, the half-man, half-beast that Picasso constantly employed in his work as a symbol of male lust and domination, comes sharply to mind. The sado-masochism of the monster lay buried deep in Picasso's psyche. It explains much of what he did to Françoise and to others. An American writer, Deborah Trustman, noted this underlying trait reflected in Picasso's portraits of Jacqueline, finding them cruelly insulting to his beautiful second wife. As Trustman wrote in the *New York Times* magazine: 'There is something destructive, brutal about them. They catch – even exploit – Jacqueline's terrible anxiety and self-effacement. Her smile is too fixed, too serene. . . . Picasso was not merciful.'

His refusal to make a will was part of the same devilishness, the final savage joke on those who would succeed him. It showed, too, his innate distrust of everyone around him, Jacqueline included. More simply, it demonstrated an intentional shirking of responsibility. Claude says: 'It was not possible for my father to make all the decisions involved. How was he going to write a will in good faith, distributing everything fairly between all of us?'

Difficulties aside, a strong suspicion remains that

Picasso's love of leg-pulls was also part of his reasoning. Paloma certainly thinks so. 'Oh, definitely. First of all, he could never even bear to think for a moment about his death. That's the first thing. Nobody likes to dwell on that. No, but some people like to prepare for what's going to happen after they die. And I think, on the contrary, he didn't want to know. He'd *rather* it was a mad problem for us to solve! I mean, the idea that it would be a crazy affair would have pleased him rather than the contrary.' She believes that her father's scorn for conventional methods also played a large part. 'He didn't like to have things on paper. He didn't have a passport for fifty or sixty years, something like that. Can you believe it? Anything that had to do with legal papers, he would rather not do.' She laughs, admitting that like her brother she herself has made a will. 'A very simple one. In a way I can understand my father's reluctance. It is rather gruesome planning what's going to happen after your death. The lawyers want you to do everything properly and you keep putting it off. In the end you never do it.'

Paloma's mother sees Picasso's action as 'a trick which misfired'. Françoise believes there are many more complex reasons for his lack of a will or statement. 'He was a very intelligent man, and he was certainly aware that he was doing something very destructive. The strange part is, I think, that he was not playing a trick so much on his future heirs – he was playing a trick on himself. It was self-destructive!'

4

THE WAYWARD SON

There were others, outsiders and friends such as William Rubin, Director of New York's Museum of Modern Art, who equally glimpsed a duality in Picasso's nature. 'He was playful,' Rubin told Milton Esterow of *ARTnews* in the summer following Picasso's death. 'He even played with people to some extent, cat and mouse.' With his own children in particular. Peter Hamill, writing in *New York* magazine went further: 'As a lover he alternated between charming rogue and brutal, indifferent monster . . . [with his children] he was doting, playful when they were young, callous as they grew up.' One of Picasso's lawyers confirmed this to Deborah Trustman: 'Picasso was not what one would call a family man. He would play with the children for a few minutes, then he forgot about them. He loved only one thing, his painting. Not his women, not his children. . . . He lived for nothing but himself.' The tragic death of Pablito, the appalling agony of mind which this inflicted on his mother and sister and all those in the family who heard the horror of the drama, stemmed largely from this.

'He could be overbearing, selfish, tyrannical, self-indulgent and on occasions brutally hard,' Patrick O'Brian wrote. 'He was, as he said himself, a man who could say *merde* to anyone on earth. As for pride, Lucifer could never have held a candle to Picasso.' Even David Douglas Duncan, the American photographer who still can't believe his luck in having been befriended and allowed valuable exclusive photography privileges by Picasso in his last seventeen years (thereby becoming the unchallenged Picasso *photographer royal*), has had to admit that his hero's dominating influence was often terrifying. 'I found it more exhausting to be with Picasso than to be in combat,' Duncan told an interviewer at the time of publication of his book *The Silent Studio*. Though Duncan had seen action with the US Army, he was often afraid of Picasso, 'constantly under the full tension of waiting for what he would do next'.

In the case of his first-born, his only legitimate child, the whole of Paulo's life had been distorted by this fluctuating tide of warmth. Between them was a bond like a cord, tugging Paulo towards the dangerous brilliance of his father's world for which he was neither mentally nor physically equipped.

Paulo was born in 1921, two years after Picasso's marriage to Olga Koklova. His early youth was spent in the globe-trotting high society of the day in pursuit of Olga's desire for fashionable flings in all the best-patronized resorts of Europe. They moved 'with the season', floating between Juan-les-Pins and Monte Carlo in summer, and the snows of Switzerland and Austria in winter. Picasso's newly found wealth and fame drew attention wherever they went. Olga demanded an incessant stream of entertainment, and Paulo shared its worst as well as its best fruits. What Françoise calls 'the international birds of paradise' were close companions of these revels: Scott and Zelda Fitzgerald, Jean Cocteau and many others less famous joined them in a round of pleasure-seeking and parties. These were the decadent pre-war years of the twenties and thirties, and Olga, dragging Picasso and their son in her wake, made the most of them. It was the fashion of the day for those who could afford it to care little for anything but the thrill of discovering new faces and places. Picasso provided his family with the funds to follow this sybaritic lifestyle, and for a time he, too, enjoyed the constant changes of scene and pace.

He was immensely proud of his dark-eyed son, painting Paulo in harlequin costume in the famous poses which became some of his best-loved if least interesting paintings. He indulged the boy, treating him like an animated doll to be displayed and put on show before his fashionable friends. The effect was crippling. When Françoise was taken to see the apartment in the rue la Boëtie in Paris where Olga and Paulo had lived with Picasso until the marriage broke up in 1935, she was astonished to see evidence of Paulo's immaturity in his room. Nothing had been touched. The room was as he had left it when he was a youth of fourteen, but instead of the sort of things a teenager might have been expected to amuse himself with, Françoise found only a collection of toy motorcars strewn over the floor where Paulo had played with them. On the walls were photographs of cycle-racing champions. Judging from the room and its pitiful contents, Paulo had never grown up.

From 1935 Picasso saw far less of his son, but the damage was done. The pampered little boy of the harlequin pictures grew into a difficult and often wayward youth. Picasso would receive harrowing accounts of Paulo's misdeeds in letters from his wife, who still refused to divorce him. Olga used Paulo as a hook, insisting that Picasso should join with her in extricating their son from whatever difficulties he had managed to become involved in.

It infuriated Picasso. While he could not blame Paulo entirely, being convinced that his mother secretly encouraged him in his folly, he despaired of the way the boy behaved, getting into constant trouble with the police and generally wasting his life. He confided to Françoise that he was fed up with his son under Olga's influence; that Paulo was lazy, lacked ambition and could not hold down a decent job. It was all the fault, he finally decided, of his wife, who was encouraging her son's bad behaviour in order to attract her husband's attention and draw him to her side while the problems were settled. At other times Picasso was affectionately disposed towards the young man, their relationship swinging in typically Spanish style between furious rows and interludes of tender warmth and shared fun. They were facially alike but otherwise linked only by their love of the bizarre, Paulo being over six foot tall and with red hair which made him seem more Russian, like his mother, than Spanish. The basic dissimilarity between him and his father was that he had none of Picasso's stamina. Paulo's health was poor whereas his father had always boasted of, and shown while working, an almost animal strength. Paulo's illnesses were a constant source of concern and irritation to Picasso, who had no time for weakness in others, or in himself.

After the war Olga took Paulo to live in Switzerland to help him get over some of his childhood illnesses. By then he had acquired a motorcycle of his own. Cars and bikes were Paulo's most enduring interest, one that Picasso indulged him in without ever being able to understand the reason for it. It simply never occurred to him that his genius as a painter and sculptor, the ease with which he could produce magnificent works of art, and the regard of his famous friends, made his way of life so unattainable to his children and grandchildren that their developing personalities took refuge in altogether less outstanding pursuits. With the exception of Paloma, whose designing talent was developed to the full, and Maya, who for a short time created beautiful pottery in her own style, Picasso's children and grandchildren were not gifted in the same way at all.

Paulo's automotive fascination was, however, completely serious. In his boyish way, he loved speed. A vehicle to him was an instrument by which he could escape temporarily from the mundane, restrictive world. With a fast car, sufficient money in his pocket to buy the drink which he could never resist, and in company with any attractive lady of whatever station in life, he felt freed from the burden of being Picasso's son. All too frequently this sense of release produced a mood of total irresponsibility, the effects of which would madden his father. Paulo's carousing, his late-night escapades with women were understood well enough by Picasso, who was no puritan. But the other crazier things in which he became involved seemed to denote the lack of any sense of native caution such as his father possessed in plenty. The boy was often absurdly reckless.

Picasso had an acquaintance in the local police force while he and Paulo and Françoise were living in Juan-les-Pins. Commissioner Isnard, as she says in her book, was a useful element in his life because he brought Picasso the local gossip which he loved to listen to. The more sordid the crime, the more Picasso revelled in the details the commissioner divulged, treating them with forensic insight. Isnard could put him in an excellent humour for the rest of the day with a really gory tale. But one night Paulo, in his usual devil-may-care way, took two girls and a man friend to a hotel opposite the police station where Isnard had his office. In the early hours of the morning ('when they had exhausted all other possibilities', as Françoise expresses it) the two men created a colossal hubbub by threatening to throw the girls out of a window on to the street. All this took place in full view of the *gendarmerie* where the police, presumably because they were aware of their commissioner's connection with the great Picasso, took no action. Next morning, however, Picasso had a visit from his friend which did not improve his humour. Isnard furiously insisted that he 'do something about your son'.

When the commissioner had gone, Picasso summoned Françoise and demanded that she bring Paulo to him right away. The young man, several inches taller than his father, was so terrified that he made Françoise go into Picasso's presence ahead of him while he tried to shield his over-six-foot frame behind her. Picasso hurled first his shoes, then books, then anything else he could lay his hands on at his wayward son. Paulo was called everything unprintable in both the French and Spanish languages. It may have chastened him at the time but did little to halt his downward path. Whatever seeds of dissolution lay in Picasso, and there were many, had been handed on to his son in large measure.

Later, and absolutely against his father's wishes, Paulo made friends with his father's chauffeur, Marcel, and was often to be seen joy-riding with him in one of Picasso's stud of great and noble motorcars. Marcel influenced him as much as anyone; the idea of being employed and paid to drive beautiful motorcars, as his friend was, appealed strongly to Paulo. Between bouts of hell-raising and drinking, Paulo was a serious student of motor racing, especially by motorcycle, and his own Norton machine was kept well tuned by Marcel with Paulo working long hours on its maintenance. When Marcel was fired for crashing one of Picasso's cars, Paulo was happy to take his job.

Two years before his father died, Paulo took another job, which gave him great pleasure and allowed him to be at the wheel of a fast motorcar travelling long distances. He and friends in Paris started an independent delivery service for newspaper and magazine publishers who would pay, so they optimistically believed, for speedy transportation of their products across Europe. Unfortunately, there were not enough clients to subsidize their efforts and the business collapsed. Financially, the loss to Paulo was unimportant. His father provided him with a small allowance which paid the rent, and Picasso had also put up the money for his share of the business partnership so he lost nothing on his own. The business's failure, though, robbed Paulo of an activity he cherished more than money: the regular driving of his beloved Citroën motorcar over long distances at high speed in dashes covering hundreds of kilometres. As he

said: 'I was driving overnight to Brussels and Lyons with
the papers. I was the delivery man and it was tremendous
fun for me. I must have covered thousands of kilometres
every week, my Citroën loaded up with papers and magazines. And I've always been keen on cars and driving so it
was just what I wanted.'

To the press reporters to whom he made these remarks,
Paulo Picasso was largely a figure of fun. His work as his
father's chauffeur and in other menial jobs gave them ready
material for stories emphasizing the wide gap between Paulo
and his famous, wealthy father. Always ready to share a
pastis or a glass of wine with a journalist hard up for a
gossipy item, Paulo became the performing monkey to his
father's much less approachable and amusing organ-
grinder.

The job he had lost had also paid 'a bit of money' –
something Paulo was never abundantly flush with. When
he married her, his second wife, Christine Pauplin, put her
small capital into the opening of a tiny boutique in the rue
du Dragon, just off the Boulevard St-Germain and a stone's
throw from their Paris home. She worked in the shop serving
the wealthy Parisians who sought out such places in pursuit
of bargains. Her customers had no idea that the woman
selling goods to them was the wife of Pablo Picasso's only
son, his one legitimate offspring and legal heir.

When Jacqueline contacted him with the news of his
father's death, Paulo was saddened but struck almost simultaneously by the momentous realization that now there
would be no more scrimping and saving for him and his
second family. He had only the haziest notion of his father's
wealth, but he was shrewd enough to know that with it he
would be well able to provide handsomely for his family in
future. It was an exciting prospect and, not surprisingly,
called for immediate celebration. Paulo was not strong-
willed. Photographs show an insignificant, somewhat
shabby figure despite his height, whose drinking set him
apart from normal society. The dark red hair was now

turning grey-white over a thin, sallow face, which bore the marks of premature ageing. He had his father's eyes, but Paulo's lacked all fire and force. He looked what he was, one of life's less successful beings.

He probably found Jacqueline's need of him flattering, if surprising. During her life with his father, when Picasso would see Paulo and make what arrangements he could to help him out of a long series of difficulties, Jacqueline had taken very little part. Now she was asking him to join her, to be her ally in the approaching battle over his father's estate. That there was to be a battle, he was left in no doubt. Paulo knew enough about his father's affairs to realize that conflict within the family, its many branches and entanglements, was inevitable. On arrival at the Mas, it can have come as no surprise to him to find Jacqueline surrounded by lawyers and papers, arming herself for the fray.

As Jacqueline explained in those first minutes, the issue now before them was a simple one: would the various (perhaps more various than they knew) factions, offspring and relatives seek to rob them of all his father had left in their care? Was it not their joint duty to his father's sacred memory to guard against incursion by the others, motivated as they were by malice and greed? This made immediate sense to Paulo, who knew all about avarice. He was still smarting from the indignities inflicted during the lawsuits brought against him by Emilienne, his first wife, in her attempts to gain more maintenance support from him. She, he knew, would seek advantage from his father's death if given the slightest opportunity. Then there was Françoise Gilot Salk and her illegitimate children. He knew his half-brother Claude and half-sister Paloma slightly. They were nice young people and always pleasant to him, but they, too, must be prevented from thwarting his rights in the inheritance. He, Paulo, was the only true son and heir. Jacqueline and his father's distinguished lawyer, Maître Roland Dumas, said so and they must be right.

Paulo's reasoning, clouded by alcohol, is not hard to follow, but from then on his behaviour was surprising. Did he take it on himself to bar his children from visiting the Mas while their grandfather's body lay there, or from attending Picasso's funeral? It is one of the more intriguing questions of *l'affaire Picasso*: who actually made the decision to keep 'the others' out?

If Paulo took it, deciding to rid himself once and for all of his irritating connection with Emilienne, his first wife – and therefore with their children – he cannot have had the least idea of the state of mind they (and especially Pablito) were in. Paulo was not ordinarily a brave man. There had been many times, for instance, when he had funked facing his father. Yet he went to the Vallauris café rendezvous determined, apparently, to give the *coup de grâce* to any notion his children might have of future gain from their grandfather's estate. A few drinks and it seems that he had all the Dutch courage needed to do this, however shocking the effect. Under no circumstances, he told them, would they share in the inheritance. His father had never wished that they should do so, and he would see to it that they did not. Their mother was equally excluded. 'You should be grateful for what has already been done for you,' he told them. Marina was scandalized. 'What have you done for us?' she cried. 'Our mother lives a wretched life. We have had no support from you for months.' Paulo shrugged. There was, he told them, nothing he could do. Jacqueline would permit nobody to see Picasso's body. She had already made arrangements for Picasso to be taken to Vauven-argues.

Paulo's justification may have been the advice of the lawyers who were assuring him that he alone, apart from Jacqueline, stood to inherit his father's wealth. It's hard to believe that he meant to do nothing for his first wife and their two children if and when he became, as seemed inevitable, so immensely rich. The suspicion, however, that he was not above hurting those who, directly or (as in

61

Pablito and Marina's case) indirectly, opposed him is hard to ignore. It would indeed be surprising if he had not inherited at least part of Picasso's genetic programming. Though Françoise had found him to be a pleasant, easy-going young man with a genial disposition, age and alcohol had begun to take their toll. Paulo was in his early fifties. A long history of bitter marital rows had had its effects. In this, as in his behaviour towards his children, there was a definite indication that he was not altogether free of the hurtful and sado-masochistic tendencies attributed to his father.

Arguably, he was capable of showing another side to those he liked and got on with. But who is not? To his father's young mistress, Geneviève Laporte, Paulo was 'good-hearted, with a kind of carefree disposition'. She saw none of the fire in him that marked Picasso's worst moods.

Geneviève, in her book *Sunshine at Midnight*, tells of a morning row between Paulo and his father over the hot water Picasso wanted for a bath which Paulo had 'stolen'. According to the author, Paulo was living then at a hotel in Paris where he lacked a bath of his own. He had taken a bath at his father's studio in rue des Grands Augustins without asking permission to do so, and Picasso was furious. 'Go and have a bath at your mother's,' Picasso is said to have raged. (Olga was by then living some sixty or so miles from Paris, in Picasso's Château de Boisgeloup near Les Andelys.) 'Go to your wife's place,' he continued. (Paulo and Emilienne were separated, as Picasso well knew.) 'Go and have a bath where you like, but I forbid you to take my water.'

Laporte says Paulo 'remained more or less unmoved by his father's outbursts of fury', but those who knew him better held Picasso as responsible as anyone for Paulo's shortcomings. On one occasion, after a bullfight his father took him to, at which Picasso delighted in receiving the bull's ears from the matador as a tribute to his distinguished presence, Paulo returned from the arena and shaved off all one side of his usually long thick hair. The underlying significance of this gesture was not lost on Françoise, who recorded it in her book.

It is impossible to absolve Paulo of all guilt for Pablito's death, or for the damaging friction that surrounded the settlement of his father's affairs. Paulo had certainly showed callous disregard for his son's feelings and situation. His behaviour towards his two eldest children strongly suggests that the court officers and social workers were not wrong in holding him responsible for much of the difficulty in his earlier marriage. But if he wronged others in the family, how much more had he himself suffered from the failure of his father to bring him up decently? The sins of the father were never more unjustly visited than upon Paulo. The simple, pretty boy with the dark Picasso eyes stares plaintively at us, dressed in his father's charming conceit of a harlequin's costume. It is as if the boy in the clown's costume senses the cruel irony behind this choice of clothes. Harlequin is a creature of laughter and tears, but rarely in equal measure. For Paulo it was to be tears all the way, his own and those of the family he could not love.

5

THE FEUD

As the weeks following Picasso's and Pablito's deaths crept by, rumours of the enormous size and complexity of Picasso's fortune began to circulate. Speculation was rife. How much would the heirs inherit and who, finally, would they be? In London, the *Observer* estimated 'some £300 million' as the value of the entire estate. There was also curiosity among the prurient concerning the likely benefit to Picasso's children, both known and unknown. Would there perhaps be some whom nobody had heard of to date? It was a pretty piece of scandal for the gossips to mull over, knowing as they did that Picasso's reputation for callousness and disregard for his own flesh and blood might well result in hitherto anonymous offspring deciding to show themselves in public now that there was money at stake. Should another child show up with convincing proof of its parentage, it could be every bit as entitled to a share in the millions as the ex-mistresses' children, Maya, Claude and Paloma.

Newspaper journalists dwelt lovingly on this possibility. The putative heirs themselves pondered the likelihood of some secret blood-claimant springing from Picasso's chequered past. 'I used to think about it,' Paloma says, widening the dark Spanish eyes that Picasso gave not only to his children, but also to the portraits of many of the women he painted, whatever their natural colour. 'I thought it might happen, that someone would get in touch with us, or with the lawyers, claiming that he or she was descended from who knows who by my father. In fact, it only happened once.' A girl in Italy approached the family, having read of the legal tussle going on over the inheritance. 'She had no proof of anything,' Paloma says, 'and the thing was soon dealt with. I don't think she had any claim, really.' Which did not entirely dispel the possibility that others might appear. Although Picasso's sequence of love affairs was well documented, his chance encounters with women of all sorts, classes and nationalities had been too numerous, and often too casual, for them all to have found their way on to a biographer's list. A particularly dangerous element in his character, it was noted, was the artist's desire to cement every sexual relationship with the birth of a child.

The catalogue of Picasso's romantic engagements reveals that there was a connection between his work and his sex-life. The staying power of each of his women seemed governed by this. When Picasso felt a need for a change of style or medium in his work, that was when customarily he would become restless in his intimate life, the moment when he would seek, and usually find, a new partner to stimulate the creative impulse in whatever direction it was taking.

As a teenager in Barcelona, then in Madrid and in Paris, the city he first came to at the turn of the century as a brilliantly precocious painter of nineteen, he was perhaps too close to the breadline to have more than fleeting encounters with women; too poor to pay more than an occasional visit to the teeming brothels of Montmartre, where he settled. The paintings he produced then, the stark and tragic 'blue period' studies, reflect emasculation rather than sexuality. It was only when he came to enjoy the delights of his first mistress, Fernande Olivier, that he expressed joy in his 'rose period' works.

Picasso and Fernande settled in Paris, enduring the most abject poverty but rejoicing in their free life among the artists and students of the *quartier*. She stuck the life for nine years, which is a tribute to her passion for him. There were apparently times when Picasso was so hard up that he could not afford shoes for the poor girl's feet and he had to do the shopping for both of them in the cobblestoned markets. Whether they tried to produce a child is not known, but seems unlikely. They had almost no social life, not even the security of knowing when and how they would next eat. Another mouth to feed would have seemed more of a threat than a happy event. There was no suggestion given by Picasso in his later accounts of life with Fernande that beginning a family had ever been considered. By the time they broke up, he was just beginning to establish himself and to make a widening circle of friends among the artists, poets and intellectuals of left-bank Paris. Perhaps they distracted him, making his impoverished love affair seem less attractive. At all events his increasing restlessness was revealed in a succession of rows and finally the end of the relationship with Fernande.

Ironically, Fernande's successor was a young girl she had invited to share a meal with them, having met her at a party in the home of Gertrude and Leo Stein. Marcelle Humbert was pretty, impressionable and receptive. Picasso, who had been straying quite a lot (the cause of many of the rows with Fernande), simply took her over. He first persuaded Marcelle, to whom he gave the pet name of 'Eva', to pose for him, painting delightful pictures of her young, fresh beauty. A short while later he installed her in his studio on the Boulevard de Clichy and declared himself passionately in love with her. Again, so far as is known, the affair was childless. And as poor Eva, who suffered from distressing angina pain and coughs all through their relationship, died at the end of 1915 the heirs had little or nothing to fear from this union. Nevertheless, Picasso's grief at her death was evidence of very strong feelings, and it seems more likely, in her case, that he would have fathered a child by her if it had been possible. He was, or seemed to be, heartbroken by his loss of her. Yet within a short time he found solace in another woman's arms, a woman who was destined neither to break with him when symptoms of restlessness recurred nor to go conveniently to an early grave.

Olga Koklova was a member of the fashionable Diaghilev ballet, a great beauty and a member of the displaced Russian upper-middle class of Tsar Nicholas. At a time when Picasso was finding in the ballet a rich seam of inspiration, she became his favourite model – with predictable results. What had been lacking in Fernande excited him in Olga, a dark, soulful and voluptuous lady. She also offered a convenient path to the social milieu which he privately despised but which increasingly provided customers for his works. Olga and her set introduced him to a circle of moneyed Parisians and artists who regarded him as 'a coming young man'.

After five years of this, he should have known better. Instead, he made the mistake of marrying this reduced-in-circumstances lady from the Russian *haute bourgeoisie* when she was about to have his child. Paulo's imminent arrival painted a false gloss of hope and fulfilment over their widely different characters. The uncharacteristically pretty paintings Picasso achieved of his son gave way to grotesque studies in which Olga was portrayed as a monster. When they parted in 1935, their marriage had been dissolved though not ended. Olga refused divorce on the grounds that they had married under Spanish law, which forbade it. Picasso turned his back on her social aspirations and took refuge in the soft arms of his next lover.

Marie-Thérèse Walter's love for Picasso is lost in obscurity but it lasted until the end of her life. Their affair originated under Olga's sharp nose, causing great unpleasantness, but Picasso was never disturbed by these womanly tirades. He saw them as inevitable in a world of 'goddesses or doormats'. It is questionable which of these he found more psychologically satisfying.

Olga was certainly no doormat. She continued to haunt his life, demanding recognition as his wife until her death in 1955. Marie-Thérèse came closer to the warm cosiness of a hearthrug, if not quite a doormat. As a model she had the flowing, aqueous lines he was using increasingly in both his paintings and his sculpture. Though blonde, in contrast to his other women, and lacking the capacity to match his sharp, quaint wit, Marie-Thérèse gave refuge to his soul as well as to his body. They first became lovers in 1927 during one of Olga's irrepressible campaigns to engage Picasso's failing interest in her endless round of parties and socially acceptable *divertissements*. In an act of rebellion, he made Marie-Thérèse pregnant, and the birth of her daughter was the final cause of the dissolution of his marriage.

Maya was born in 1935, the year Picasso left his wife to preside in solitary state over her tea table. He then moved in with Marie-Thérèse, but remained living with her for a bare year before their baby was born, though revisiting them on and off for years afterwards. Why he did not stay longer is partly explained by the advent of another, very different, woman, Dora Maar. Here was a dynamic and beautiful individual whose attractions did not begin and end in bed, or on the modelling couch. Dora was an artist and photographer from Yugoslavia, dark, passionate, witty and intelligent. Their affair lasted from 1936 until 1943, and she is to be seen in Picasso's vast black and white masterpiece, *Guernica*, painted in passionate reaction to German bombing during the Spanish Civil War. Prophetically, Dora Maar is portrayed as a woman weeping for a lost lover.

Marie-Thérèse left Picasso on the day she discovered that Dora Maar's interest in him, ostensibly photographic, was better developed than any film. She and Picasso remained occasional lovers, pride preventing her from admitting to the encroachment of a rival, but the loss of Picasso as a constant companion may have affected Marie-Thérèse's mind. For several of her earliest years, Maya's mother kept up the fiction that he was still living with them, telling the child to be quiet 'as your father is working upstairs'. A room which he used as a studio at the top of Maya's grandmother's house, where they lived, was kept permanently locked, though Picasso was only an infrequent visitor. In the family it is generally believed that Marie-Thérèse fostered this illusion for her daughter's sake, but Maya loyally refuses to accept this. 'My father was always coming to visit us and stay with us, all his life,' she maintains. 'He and my mother shared a love nothing could destroy.'

She would visit her father in his studio in the rue des Grands Augustins and they would speak to each other in Spanish, which few of the visitors understood. 'We'd chat about his women friends without them knowing, which was crazy,' she says. At a time when her mother and Dora Maar were competing for Picasso's affection, it must also have been very revealing. Maya claims to have shared this privileged insight into Picasso's intimate world until she reached the age of twenty, when she felt that she had to break free. 'As a young girl, I'd sit on the stairs in my grandmother's house in Paris, where he occasionally worked, and listen to him talking to women. When I got too old for that sort of thing, it was time to go.' Earlier she had complained to her father about his relations with Dora Maar, and how upsetting they were to her mother. She claims that as a result he never asked Dora to his studio again.

Certainly the gap between the two women, Marie-Thérèse and Dora Maar, was wide in terms of both intellect and sophistication. Dora was travelled, entertaining and amusing. Marie-Thérèse was thought to possess a vague and uncertain personality which bordered on the neurotic. Picasso's tenderness for her was largely physical and aesthetic, the warm curves and loops of his many studies of her expressing more clearly than words the nature of the attraction she held for him. And with Dora, whom Picasso regarded as a charming plaything, there were no children. She was a free spirit, caring for no such ties. Françoise Gilot, who was to succeed both Dora and Marie-Thérèse, noted a rigidity in her which reminded her of an ancient French expression: 'She carried herself like the holy sacrament.' No doubt Picasso's interest in her was more earthy.

The long affair with Françoise Gilot, whom he first met in Paris when she was a young art student in the early days of the Second World War, was Picasso's most mature match. She and the woman who succeeded her, Jacqueline Roque, filled his latter days from the start of his sixties until his death at the age of ninety-one. Without Françoise's children, and Jacqueline's unfortunate lack of them, there would have been no dispute, no bitter wrangling, over the succession to his great wealth. The jealousy and rivalry between the two women, each in her own way strong and influential in affecting the framework of Picasso's life, were the foundation of the feud that followed his death.

Françoise had been Picasso's constant companion for seven years, in Paris and latterly in the South of France where he had bought the villa La Californie in Cannes, when one day they were approached on the beach by a couple called Ramié, middle-aged and commercially minded. Georges and Suzanne Ramié ran a gallery in Vallauris, the Madoura, where they made and sold pottery. Seizing her moment, Madame Ramié immediately tried to lure Picasso into paying them a visit, urging him to try his hand at designing and making ceramics. The craft offered an exciting new medium for an artist of his calibre, she explained, one equally as creative as drawing, painting or sculpture. Any ceramic designs he produced would be true 'Picassos'. Françoise took an immediate dislike to Madame Ramié, but Picasso listened to her attentively. He agreed to drive over one afternoon to the gallery, if only to satisfy his curiosity. Maybe there would be something new for him in ceramics. In his restless frame of mind at the time, it seemed worth a try.

Françoise, already aware of the threat posed by Picasso's growing boredom, could only encourage and support his enthusiastic impulse. They were driven over – Picasso never learnt how to drive – and the Ramiés soon had Picasso drawing fish, eels and sea urchins on fired clay. The results in their unglazed state were disappointing, and Picasso was eager to see the final effect. As it was impossible to arrange this immediately, he left the gallery and might well have forgotten the experiment altogether had not he and Françoise again bumped into the Ramiés in the following summer of 1947. They asked if he would like to see his completed work. He was delighted to find it transformed, the colours warm, rich and glowing. The first 'Picasso pots' entranced him and opened up an entire new avenue of shape and form.

Françoise felt pleased when her lover steeped himself in this new activity. Quite soon he was producing at the gallery a range of original works of astonishing variety and beauty. Françoise should perhaps have guessed that this activity would bring a new woman into his life but as the mother of his babies, now growing to infancy, she may have felt secure against newcomers.

Every summer for five years Picasso continued developing this new art form, mastering every known technique and continually inventing fresh and fascinating forms. Then, in 1952, the Ramiés announced that, needing someone to help in the gallery, they had invited their young cousin, Jacqueline Roque, recently divorced from an engineer called Hutin, to take on the job. She and her daughter Catherine were living in a small villa between Golfe-Juan and Juan-les-Pins called Le Ziquet – in Provençal dialect 'the little goat', as Françoise sharply pointed out. Picasso was introduced to Jacqueline and found her young, beautiful and sympathetic. He became a regular visitor to her home.

That winter the gallery was unusually quiet. Jacqueline found plenty of time to cultivate Picasso, to learn his often demanding ways. Contact with him when he was on an artistic 'high' was an inflammable situation for a young and beautiful girl, as Françoise herself should have remembered. The relationship nevertheless ripened while, surprisingly, his mistress seemed scarcely to have given it a thought. Perhaps it was because she had known so many 'other women' in his life; too many to worry her head over one young girl at a gallery. A year or so before, Picasso had begun a passing affair with a seventeen-year-old Parisian girl, Geneviève Laporte. His loyalty to Françoise wavered occasionally, she knew, but she felt no serious qualms about him now that she had his children.

Even when his irritability and irrational changes of mood led to friction and rows between them, she saw no threat from the dark-haired Jacqueline. The younger woman was welcomed by her whenever Picasso, as he often did, brought her home with him. Jacqueline slowly became part of his working life, as other women always had been and always would be. Jealousy was not an emotion Françoise allowed herself to feel, and anyway there seemed no cause for it. But her own relationship with him was no longer what it had been. Her 'sacred monster' had become a brute who did his best to savage her with words. When she could stand no more of his vindictive attacks, she fled to Paris, seeking at least a respite. She took the children with her. Only when she returned did Françoise realize the extent of her mistake.

Jacqueline Roque was installed in her place. Françoise's clothes were still in the wardrobes; Jacqueline had been wearing them. Picasso, most plainly, was no longer Françoise's lover and protector, merely the father of their children. Her life with him was over, and she could blame nobody but Jacqueline. Françoise stayed on a while, putting up with her conqueror's daily visits for the sake of the children, but now she must endure a secondary role in what she had called Picasso's 'kingdom'. She was no longer its queen.

When she eventually surrendered the keys, her successor had already taken full possession of the house. All that was left to the mistress who had given Picasso the two children he professed to love so dearly, and whom he had painted in their infancy so touchingly, was her memories. 'Whatever you do from now on, your life will be lived before a mirror that will throw back at you everything you have lived through with me, because each of us carries around with him the weight of his past experiences,' Picasso told her sententiously. It was that sentence which prompted her to begin her chronicle of life with him, the book she called *Life with Picasso*. In doing so, had she realized it, she was handing Jacqueline the ultimate weapon.

The book, written in collaboration with a distinguished American art critic, Carlton Lake, was unreservedly frank. Françoise wrote: 'Until now I had seen him, through his inner life, as a unique phenomenon. But now in his seventies I saw him spending his energies in the most frivolous and irresponsible ways. I saw him for the first time from outside. . . . And all the standards he had set up and so carefully observed were thrown aside. . . .

'"You won't last as long as I will," he told me. He couldn't seem to bear the idea that anyone who had been part of his life should survive him. I recalled how he told me at the beginning, "Every time I change wives I should burn the last one. That way I'd be rid of them. They wouldn't be around now to complicate my existence. Maybe that would bring back my youth, too. You kill the woman and you wipe out the past she represents."'

The book was scrupulously fair to her successor. Françoise managed to make Jacqueline sound like the nurse of fiction who steals the heart of the wounded warrior. In the few passages showing the three of them together, Jacqueline is described weeping with frustration when Picasso refuses to accept her views on the bullfight, tears streaming down her face while she pathetically wipes them and her hair out of her eyes. Françoise stands aloof, refusing to begin a fight she knows she cannot win. Picasso's classification of women as 'goddesses or doormats' was never more vividly portrayed.

The book won almost universal praise except for reviews like that in *The Times*, which obviously considered anything so frank to be irredeemably 'vulgar'. In the *Observer*, Arthur Koestler noted sympathetically that the book demonstrated 'a mathematical proof: so much goodwill on both sides, and all in vain'. Koestler recalled the passage where, having come into Picasso's life as 'a rather prim virgin of twenty-one', Françoise showed how her self-control – 'all my life I had been warned away from public displays or emotions' – could tantalize Picasso. 'When I shout at you and say disagreeable things, it's to toughen you up,' she reported her lover as shouting at her in fury. 'I'd like you to get angry, shout and carry on, but you don't. I'd like just once to see you spill your guts out on the table, laugh, cry – play *my* game.'

A dangerous game indeed, but no more so than the effect of publishing the book. Those outside her circle of friends believe it enabled Jacqueline to create, in Emilienne's words, 'a vacuum around Picasso'. Under Jacqueline's protection, it was impossible to gauge how many of his subsequent actions were his alone, and how many were prompted by her.

Marie-Thérèse maintained at the time that Jacqueline had 'wrought a fundamental change' in her old lover. In the admiring view of her friends Jacqueline was 'a saint' who loved and watched over Picasso like a guardian angel, but others in the family were less charitable. 'She kept him as though in prison,' Emilienne has said. 'That was her whole existence, she thought of nothing else.' Emilienne's daughter, Marina, echoes this more forcefully. 'After the marriage, my grandfather seemed to lose his humanity. We saw absolutely nothing of him, we received absolutely nothing from him. My feeling is that most of that must have originated with Jacqueline; it could have come from no-one else.'

To Françoise, the attack Picasso subsequently made on the book, whether or not it was inspired by Jacqueline, was astounding. 'I had been careful never to make any statement in it which I could not substantiate with absolute proof, even with letters which I had at the time. Yet he attacked it, saying it was full of lies!' When Picasso brought a legal action against Calman Levy, her publishers, in 1964, Françoise was forced to provide documentation to substantiate her claims. Picasso lost the case in the lower court, then took it to appeal and lost again.

As Françoise says: 'It had already been proved that what I said was true. The appeal judge now had to decide on an altogether different aspect of the case. His point was: "Yes, it is true, but is it indiscreet?" Our lawyers argued that the ten years we had spent together constituted a *community of fact*. If Pablo could sue me for writing the book, then for all the portraits that he had painted of me with my nose on the wrong side and so on, I would be able to sue him. If he was entitled to his version of the facts, then so was I.' Again, and this time finally, Picasso lost the case. Françoise's evidence had ridiculed his claim. As she says: 'The book was *not* indiscreet, because Pablo had made a habit of living his entire life in a glasshouse. He wasn't the slightest bit averse to publicity, and this applied equally to his so-called private life.'

So Picasso and Jacqueline could go no further. If their intention had been to reduce the impact of the book, to play down the public's conception of Françoise's role in Picasso's life, they had achieved the exact opposite. The publicity surrounding Picasso's action against Françoise ensured that she was now a famous woman, the cast-off mistress of a celebrated artist.

When Picasso congratulated her on her successful defence, Françoise could have accused him of using the whole

costly court action to make a stupid and vindictive attack
on her, but she knew very well who was responsible.
'[Jacqueline] had a Lady Macbeth complex,' Françoise
declares. 'Even though Lady Macbeth did not do those
things herself, she introduced them into Macbeth's soul.'
The manipulative genius which Shakespeare's heroine
shows was echoed, Françoise believes, in Jacqueline.
'Shakespeare was a good psychologist. He had knowledge
of the human soul. In Jacqueline's psychological make-up,
if you look at it closely, you will see that there is a parallel
to the Macbeth situation. To me, she is slightly megalo-
maniac.'

Jacqueline now faced the unenviable task of comforting
the loser, a man who could not abide defeat despite his
cheery words of congratulation to Françoise. However much
or little she had encouraged Picasso to mount this futile
attack, however much she would continue to denounce the
book as 'discredited' and 'vulgar', her rivalry had ensured
its success. Jacqueline had misjudged the strength of the
opposition. Blinded perhaps by the adulation she felt for
Picasso's genius, she had prompted him in all good faith to
fight the losing battle. Forty-five years in age separated her
from him, but there was another, perhaps greater, gulf
between them, that of understanding. Françoise had a
definite advantage there.

Nevertheless, in his old age – he was by now in his eighties
– the 'doormat' was more in demand than the goddess.
Jacqueline's subservience to his every need and whim was
a constant stimulation to Picasso's waning energies. And
perhaps, when all is said and done, her natural reluctance
to share him with his previous mistress, despite the cost of
two unsuccessful actions, was flattering.

Jacqueline has always declared that it was the book that
turned Picasso against the children, causing what French
journalist Nicolas Adam called 'the final break in the family'. She voiced her own disgusted reaction to it and talked
openly of her husband's distress over it. Friends like David

Duncan and his wife, their American neighbours, listened sympathetically when she complained of the 'invasion of Pablo's privacy'. The general opinion of both friends and family, however, was that whether or not Picasso had read the enjoyable, well-written story Jacqueline had poisoned his mind against both it and its author.

Following the failure of Picasso's action on appeal, it seemed the most that he and Jacqueline could do to thwart Françoise and her children in their fight to be duly recognized was to foster the belief that *Life with Picasso* was a vulgar and catchpenny intrusion into the life of a great man which had caused him distress. Then in the spring of 1964 both children were told, abruptly and without explanation, that they were no longer welcome at their father's home. For ten years until then, recognized as his children and bearing his name, they had spent holidays at Christmas and in summer with him and Jacqueline. Now, apparently, their father wished for no further contact with them. Only once, on his own admission, did Claude Picasso encounter his father in the flesh after the barriers went up. 'We happened to pass each other in the street in Cannes one day,' he told Peter Lewis of the *Daily Mail*. 'We spoke for about a minute before he passed on. He was with my stepmother, of course.' One is left to wonder what can have been said.

Jacqueline and others blamed the book for his estrangement, but Françoise knew that the rift had started well before it was published. It could not possibly have been the cause of Picasso's animosity towards his children. In her considered opinion, that could only have been produced and encouraged by Jacqueline. 'She confused people. She said it was "on account of my abominable book". All nonsense! It is not abominable at all. It is very nice to Pablo. Anyway, she made it appear that the children had been rejected *because* of it. Whereas, they were rejected after they had acquired their father's name, which is quite a different story. And that's the truth.'

The legal victory gave Françoise the right to publish her story anywhere in the world. *Life with Picasso* became a bestseller, a Book of the Month selection in the United States, and a widely discussed work. It left on record the intimate story of Picasso's life as both lover and father. More important still, the tried and tested status of the book's statements about her children's parentage provided a keynote in Françoise's campaign to ensure Claude and Paloma's rights of succession. 'I had set up a trust, the *conseil de famille*, on the children's behalf, with Picasso as a trustee. That and the maintenance payments he was making for them kept a sort of distant relationship going between us. It at least showed that Picasso had acknowledged the children were his, which was most important.'

But when she filed a suit to establish their rights to inherit, he opposed it. Picasso had allowed them the use of his name, now Maître Dumas was instructed to fight against any right of inheritance. Late in 1970 he succeeded in having the case thrown out of the small provincial court of Grasse. As Picasso said to a somewhat baffled court reporter after the hearing: 'They have my name. Isn't that enough?' Françoise Gilot did not think it was.

After his death, she made an urgent reassessment of her departed lover's motives. She was still uncertain to what extent he had planned the imbroglio her children were involved in, but it was clear to her that she was the root cause of Picasso's mischief. 'I saw that it was *our* fight, the tug-of-war between us, which had set the scene. Pablo was determined to do this to me after his death, since he had failed to do it while he was alive. In that context it became clear to me that the struggle between us had been more important than our love affair.' She also recognized that Jacqueline, the usurper of her place in Picasso's life, had influenced Picasso in ways which materially affected her children. The refusal to let them share in their father's funeral, or even enter his house after he died, was a stinging insult, but it was the recollection of all the years until now when they had been turned away from his door without explanation that really burned. In Françoise's eyes, Jacqueline had played a leading part in this for no other reason than her desire to expunge all reminders of his former mistress.

Françoise's first act upon hearing of Picasso's death was therefore to urge Claude and Paloma to continue to press their rightful claims against the estate as determinedly as she had pressed them against Picasso during his lifetime while they were minors. From her home in California she kept in close touch with the unfolding drama, furious at Paulo's dismissal of his own children and saddened by Pablito's senseless suicide, but increasingly seeing Jacqueline as the biggest obstacle in her children's path. The widow's refusal to let them share in their father's funeral was the last straw, strengthening Françoise's determination to see that Jacqueline did not trample over everything she had gained for her children. In doing this, she appears not to have worried that her actions might be construed as petty spite, or the jealousy of a deposed mistress. She sought only to complete a task she had set herself when life with Picasso became unbearable. Then he seemed to have betrayed all the trust she had put in his assurances. She substituted Jacqueline for Picasso now because she believed the widow had, as she put it to her children, 'used undue influence' over him.

Françoise's supreme coolness in fighting for her children's rights impressed both of them, especially Paloma. It made her confident. And later, when she was more mature, she adopted the attitude: 'well, as I have all the convenience of being Picasso's daughter, I may as well use that as a tool.' If that was the weapon which had been used against her, let it also be the strength on which she would build her career. Claude, on the other hand, took a somewhat different view of their destiny. He had been born with a genetic heart defect, a narrowing of the pulmonary artery, which made it necessary for him to take extra care in everything he did.

As a child he had not been allowed to join in normal games, the rough-and-tumble of school and adolescent life. His mother believes that this enhanced the disparity between her two children, augmenting the existing difference in looks and character between them. 'Paloma has a lot of her father's characteristics: the strength, the taste for power. She looks like Picasso's sister, Lola; whereas Claude, who looks more like his father physically than she does, is much more like me inside. Though he is now thirty-nine, he is still not so assured as Paloma who is nearly three years younger.'

Françoise had now divorced Luc Simon and had remarried. Her second husband was the distinguished, Nobel Prize-winning discoverer of anti-polio vaccine, Dr Jonas Salk. His support helped her to continue the fight. He maintained that the children's 'sacred monster' of a father had done terrible things to their wellbeing and self-esteem. Perhaps everyone had forgotten, the great scientist said, that Picasso had named his daughter Paloma after the celebrated 'dove of peace'. The irony of his later behaviour towards her was, in Dr Salk's eyes, 'simply incomprehensible'. As he said with feeling: 'The refusal to permit his own children to see their father or to bid him farewell was shocking, an indignity to the dead as well as to the living.'

Françoise had, besides, found a 'friendly and wise counsellor in Gaston Bouthoul, a lawyer who, though old [he died in 1980], was completely trustworthy. He advised that there was a loophole in Picasso's case to deny Claude and Paloma rights of succession, he said we must not be too Utopian, but it was worth pressing on. This was good to hear at a time when it seemed everything was against us and Pablo was at his most hostile.' After Picasso's death, Françoise no longer waged the battle herself but referred the children to Bouthoul's loophole, which seemed to be valid.

They had fought to establish their right to a place in

Picasso's succession at a time when their ages would have enabled them to qualify under the terms of the subsequent 1972 Act. As has been said, this Act establishes the legal rights of inheritance of *enfants adulterins* if descent is proven within two years of the illegitimate child's twenty-first birthday. Since the Act had been passing through the legislature while the case to establish the children's rights of succession was being unsuccessfully fought the first time, and since Bouthoul had craftily registered a request for exemption from the new Act's age-rule once it was passed, he felt sure that, had Picasso's death not forced them to postpone their action, Claude and Paloma would by now have overturned the judge's earlier decision on appeal.

Since Jacqueline now exercised control over everything, the danger as Françoise saw it was that the widow would override all the advantages which the mistress had won for Claude and Paloma, and latterly for Maya also, during their minority. It was no longer possible for her to act for them directly as they were of age, but she was determined that her legal experience and competence would still guide them. 'They hadn't been very hot on what I was doing, but I thought I could see further ahead than they could. When Claude reached the age of twenty-one I had filed a suit giving him the right to claim exclusion from the age barrier affecting claimants under the new Act. This was well before the Act was passed but it stood him in stead later. The same thing was true for Paloma. But I knew if they didn't handle things in the right way now that their father was dead, it might come to nothing.'

Françoise had always believed the illegitimacy label was most unjust. 'Under French law at that time, even if Picasso had been free to marry me and had done so, the children would not have been legitimized, because Olga, his ex-wife, would still have been alive.' This unfairness was the crux of her campaign to have a change made in the law. In January 1972, when the new Act came into force, giving far greater rights to children born out of wedlock, she had the

Warning sign forbidding entry to the Château de Vauvenargues.

Picasso's burial place: the Château de Vauvenargues.

Picasso's villa at Mougins where he lived with Jacqueline.
His studio is on the left.

Self-portrait of Picasso painted in Barcelona, 1896.

Picasso aged 15, 1896.

Portrait of Olga in an armchair by Picasso, 1917.

Picasso and his first wife, Olga Koklova, at the opening of 'Parade' in Paris, 1917.

Paulo Picasso (left) with his father.

Paulo with (left to right) his step-brother and sister, Claude and Paloma Picasso.

Right: Paulo as 'Harlequin' by Picasso, 192-

Above: Pablito Picasso with his grandfathe

Above left: Marina and Emilienne Picass
at Paulo Picasso's funeral in Paris, 1976.
Paloma Picasso can be seen
behind Marina.

Left: Emilienne Picasso, 1985.

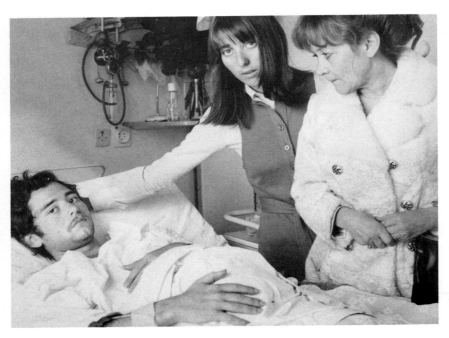

*Pablito in hospital after his suicide attempt with
(left to right) Marina and Emilienne.*

*At Pablito's funeral. From left to right Paloma,
Emilienne and Marina Picasso.*

The drawing room of 'La Californie',
Picasso's villa in Cannes as restored
by Marina.

Marina with her children Flore (left)
and Gaël (right), 1985.

Maya Widmaier, 1985.

Bernard Picasso with his mother,
Christine.

Picasso with baby Claude and Françoise, near Vallauris, 1948.

Below left: Claude posing beside one of his own drawings, 1953.

Below right: Claude with his first wife Sara, 1970.

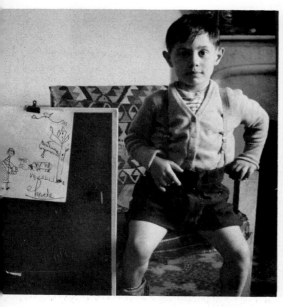

*: Claude with Sydney, his second
*, at the opening of the Picasso
*spective exhibition in the Museum
Modern Art, New York, 1980.

*Right: Picasso with Claude and
Paloma at Antibes.*

*Paloma with her husband Rafael Lopez Sanchez
at a gala opening in Paris, 1978.*

*Françoise Gilot Salk just after
the publication of her book,*
My Life With Picasso, *1965.*

Françoise, 1985.

Picasso with Jacqueline just after their marriage, at the opening of an exhibition of his works at a Cannes gallery, 1961.

Picasso and Jacqueline in the studio at Mougins.

Picasso with Brigitte Bardot in his studio.

Picasso by Man Ray, 1935.

Jacqueline by Cecil Beaton, 1965.

Roland Dumas.

Picasso with Jacqueline and his portrait of her.

satisfaction of knowing that her efforts had been successful.
Picasso's death had forced her children to postpone their
legal attempts to establish their rights, but as soon as they
re-entered their cases, claiming absolute rights under the
new law to a place in the succession, Jacqueline opposed
them. The battle between the widow and the mistress was
on.

Thus in the heat of that summer of 1973, while holiday
crowds lolled on beaches and along streets in Golfe-Juan
and nearby Cap d'Antibes and a fierce sun beat down on
Pablito's grave, the drama over the succession to the world's
richest art legacy settled into a trial of strength.

On the one hand Jacqueline and Paulo, her willing ally,
made haste to remove all works from the many homes and
hiding places where Picasso had stashed them. Those who
saw and knew – as Jacqueline did not – the relative value
of each painting, each sculpture or ceramic work, each
drawing or etching, were surprised at the selectivity with
which this fully representative collection had been assembled by its creator. Each of his famous 'periods' was
represented by a masterpiece. It was astonishing to find
such documentation because Picasso had seemed in life to
be so casual about his work. When pigeons' droppings
descended on canvases he would insist on leaving the guano
where it fell, 'giving the painting a natural flavour' he would
say. Dust had been allowed to settle thickly on many of the
works. Some of his locked rooms and houses contained
priceless paintings which he had not seen (although he was
aware of the precise location of each) for thirty and more
years. Insured for 3,000 million francs, and in guarded vans,
many of these were now conveyed by night to Paris bank
vaults and stored away. Whoever was going to benefit from
this vast haul would not do so by light-fingered acquisition.
Jacqueline, guided by Dumas, was avoiding any risk of
misappropriation of her husband's treasures.

On the other hand Françoise and to a lesser extent
Marie-Thérèse Walter were planning concerted action.

Picasso's death had temporarily halted Claude and Paloma's campaign to establish their rights to inherit, causing a frustrating delay, but this could and would be rectified. For Marie-Thérèse, the death of her great passion, the man she had loved as life itself, was too overwhelming to allow any consideration of material advantages for herself or her daughter. For her, as she well knew, there was to be no part offered (or to which she was legally entitled) in the succession. For her daughter Maya, married and with three children to bring up, it was an altogether different matter. 'She *still* did not have the right to use her father's name,' Françoise says. 'Gaston Bouthoul, the lawyer I had recommended her to use, had built up a rather good dossier for her, which was a great help. And my book was also useful because I had mentioned her in it, and it showed that Picasso had held her in esteem as his own daughter.'

At the time of their father's death it is doubtful if either Claude or Paloma, and almost certainly Maya, held any hope of receiving much at all from his great fortune. To inherit as established, rightful heirs seemed no more than a remote possibility. At the time, Maya was married and bringing up her children in Marseilles, Paloma was in Paris trying to promote herself as a designer of jewellery, and Claude had found his way to New York where he was working very successfully as a freelance photographer regularly assigned by *Life* magazine and others. He had already married and divorced. Both he and his sister were involved in the business of making an independent life, free of a father who seemed to have rejected them completely.

Jacqueline had withdrawn from any contact with the illegitimate branches of the family. She was hiding behind lawyer's robes, refusing to meet or answer the telephone to her husband's cast-off blood relations. Her attempts to ride roughshod over Claude and Paloma, assuming complete control over everything in spite of the lack of any will or testament to indicate Picasso's wishes, reached them through lawyer's letters and phone calls and aroused in

Françoise a cold anger. If Jacqueline could follow Picasso in using lawyers like heavy guns to blast out her foes, so could Françoise. By advising Claude and Paloma to demand the introduction of an official administrator she gave the first clear indication of her plan of campaign. She then bent all her energies to the task of finding lawyers and counsellors who would serve as their front-line battalions. French law, as she well knew, was muddled. Children had prior right of inheritance except when they were born out of wedlock, the issue of an unmarried relationship while the married partner was still alive. If that was the case, they lost all status as heirs.

In January 1972, however, the lock of this impenetrable barrier to Claude, Paloma and Maya's ever inheriting their father's fortune had been broken wide open by the new Act. The effect was to give all children the same rights on the death of a parent, though in varying degree and subject to proof of descent being established between the previously mentioned ages of twenty-one and twenty-three. Thereafter illegitimate offspring would receive a judiciously awarded fraction of the legitimate heirs' portion. Thus, provided they could establish their claim to share in the succession, Maya, Claude and Paloma were entitled to receive at least a part of what Picasso's legitimate offspring – Paulo, or on his death his children, Marina and Bernard – would get.

How Picasso would have viewed this was a question nobody in or out of the family could answer. He had left nothing to indicate his reaction to the new legislation. Nor had he altered his opposition to these 'naughty children' sharing in the succession, despite the fact that all that he and his lawyers had done to thwart the *adulterins* had been destroyed by the change in the law.

Françoise is sure that it met with stern disfavour from Jacqueline, whose attitude to money was often as peculiar as the belief she apparently clung to – giving many hints of it to the occasional visitors she allowed to penetrate the barricades of her retreat – that she was able to maintain spiritual communication with her dead husband. 'She has been bad to my children, and sometimes almost worse to her own daughter, Catherine,' Françoise says, 'but worst of all was her extraordinary concept of their future poverty.' She tells how, when Claude and Paloma were in their early teens and during the days when Picasso was still letting them spend holidays with him and his wife, Jacqueline took the three children to a cheap local supermarket. It was a nice morning, a typically South-of-France day of warm lazy sunshine, and the children wanted ice creams. Jacqueline had more important things on her mind than ice creams.

'She told them' – Françoise sounds astonished as she recalls the tale – "I am taking you here, the three of you, because I want you to get to know that this is the place where you should get all your costumes and clothes and things like that." Claude and Paloma said: "But we don't need such things from you. Our mother provides our clothes. So you don't have to bother. And anyway our mother doesn't buy them at a place like this."

'Jacqueline said: "Yes, I know. But that is the reason I brought you here. Because when you are grown up this is where you will have to go. The three of you." My children told me about it afterwards. They couldn't understand anything so bizarre. They asked me "Isn't she crazy?" And this was when Jacqueline was already married to their father so it was ridiculous to think that any of them, especially her own daughter, would ever have to do that. My children, even if they never saw a penny of their father's money, would certainly not have to. I would see to that. No, she was just trying to humiliate them, to be unpleasant.'

Jacqueline appeared to hold all the cards, being in possession of the estate as caretaker for the band of professionals and officials increasingly involved. Where Françoise scored was in having studied both law and psychology and in having trained and been recognized as an artist in her own right. 'Jacqueline did not really know anything about serious art,' Françoise says. 'All her whims, hypochondria or whatever, were entirely irrational.' The need to know the value of 'Picasso's Picassos', the collection he had made with such great care throughout his life of his own works, was becoming increasingly necessary.

Françoise's experience of Picasso's work had practical advantages during her life with him, which began in Paris early in the Second World War. Picasso was frustrated, shut up in the beleaguered capital and prohibited from selling his pictures. After she went to live with him Françoise was able to help him in dealing with the agents and others who timidly approached Picasso. She guided him in many ways which taught her about the commercial value of his work. His gratitude to her was expressed in his paintings. He likened her to a flower, painted her in Klee-like lines as *La Femme Fleur*, and assured her that their children, when they came, would keep their love eternally alive. She knew nothing of the habitual restlessness of his roving nature. Only Jacqueline, who took over when Françoise left him, was able to stay the course, finally outliving even his capricious desires. At the start of their conjugal relationship, however, Picasso was approaching eighty years of age and his virility was under threat from the disease which four years later resulted in prostatic surgery.

Picasso's early pictures of Jacqueline reveal a tenderness rarely shown in his later studies of women. His first painting, done in 1954, set her among roses. In the last impotent years the canvases which came incessantly from his studio held more of disgust and envy than of love. The restlessness may have been there, but the ability to pursue a fresh course had gone. Forty-five years his junior, Jacqueline was a gentle impressionable young woman with a Norman cast to her delicate unlined face. Her brow flowed directly into a long straight nose which conveyed an expression of cultured disdain. Picasso's son Paulo was five years older, but such anomalies of age had never been visible to Picasso's eye. If she could have borne Picasso's child Jacqueline would have secured the succession beyond dispute, but there were to be no more Picasso children. The removal of his 'gland of life' forced the old lion into involuntary and unwelcome retirement, leaving the empty places in the jigsaw for his mischievous exploitation.

At this time his greatest fear, driving a wedge between him and those who loved him, was that nobody would succeed him who understood or cared sufficiently for his *œuvre*, his life's work. In a candid moment in his Grands Augustins studio one sunny afternoon Geneviève Laporte says he told her: 'If I knew how much time remained to me in this life, I would send for a truck and give you everything I treasure. Do you think my heirs are capable of reorganizing the real value of things? No . . . they'll sell everything.' He trusted fewer and fewer of those around him, and restricted his circle increasingly to those whom he believed had no claim on him. Paulo was weak, ailing, and had never shown a trace of the ability and discernment, let alone the refinement of culture and taste, necessary to control such a bequest. Jacqueline knew little of art, though she cared for him and his works immaculately. She was all that he had, a willing learner, untiring and caring in cataloguing and photographing the canvases, sculptures and ceramics which flowed from his hands. She was the prop he needed, a pure-shaped vase for his genius. If he could not love her, he could and did feel something akin to that emotion, a mixture of pity and gratitude. Her resistance against the world formed a barrier when he most needed one.

The *froideur* which followed the publication of *Life with Picasso* is not the only indication of the depth of Jacqueline's animosity towards Françoise. The attractive Musée Picasso in Antibes is only a few kilometres from Jacqueline's home in Mougins, and yet she has never set foot inside it. According to the museum's curator, Danielle Giraudy, she never will because the works it contains all celebrate the years Françoise spent with Picasso. Madame Giraudy believes

Jacqueline cannot bring herself to visit her rival's monument even though it contains a wonderful selection of Picasso's works. 'She wants nothing to do with it. She knows it contains everything to do with Françoise,' the curator says. Who can assess a wife's feelings when her husband's ex-mistress is in open and public conflict with his estate? When *she*, the mistress, has the children denied the wife in marriage, and is waging an aggressive, insidious campaign on their behalf? The stage was set for a battle of classic proportions. There was immense wealth at stake, and also the satisfaction of settling, once and for all, the long-standing feud between the mistress and the wife.

6

CLAUDE AND PALOMA

If Françoise Gilot needed an excuse for doing battle on her children's behalf, the memory of Picasso's treatment of them during his marriage to Jacqueline provided it in full measure. Claude told her many times how hurt he had been by his father's unexplained rejection of Paloma and himself. 'It was always the same – my own father was too busy to see us!' The plight of this son of hers, born with a congenital heart defect and in need of special care all through his early life, wounded her. She found it hard, ultimately, to think of the man she had loved and given herself to with anything but anguish.

On one particular occasion, Claude confided, he had made a last attempt to bridge the gap. It was soon after his marriage in New York, and Sara, his young American wife, was naturally curious and anxious to meet his famous father. To please her, Claude arranged what he hoped would be a reconciliation with Picasso on a visit to the South of France. The attempt ended in humiliating failure.

Sara Lee Schultz, now Sara Lavner, was a year or two older than Claude. There could hardly have been a wider difference in background. Her family were Jewish émigrés living in Brooklyn, her father a foreman in a glitter factory. Totally unsophisticated, her mother had never heard of Picasso. 'What is your name, Picass-i-o?' she asked Claude at their first meeting. In other areas, too, they were miles apart. Sara was a bubbling pretty blonde student at Brooklyn College who had recently swapped from studying psychology to stagecraft. Claude had inched himself into a reasonably top bracket in New York as a freelance photographer. That was after Richard Avedon, who had once taken pictures of him in Paris, had given him a start working in his own studio. Sara was hopeless as a housewife, she says, but Claude liked helping with practical, domestic chores. 'My mother had brought me up like a retarded princess,' she explains. 'She would never let me wash a dish. Claude had to teach me how to boil water, I couldn't do a thing.'

They lived together in Brooklyn for a 'lovely' year before he asked her to marry him. She instinctively felt it was unlikely to last, but the chance to become Madame Picasso was too good to miss. His dark good looks and charm were very appealing, and to their friends they seemed equally in love. Françoise would have preferred it if they had continued to live together rather than marry because she knew the long-lasting effect which his father's rejection had had on her son. She had seen it hinder him in school work and noted the onset of a cycle of depressive moods. 'Claude was struggling to take his "*bac*" (matriculation) examination at the time Picasso shut him out of his life. It left him very upset and I felt he needed time to settle his own mind before he married.'

Françoise had done all she could. She took Claude with her to England where she believed he would benefit from a complete change and the company of people who had, in her opinion, a calmer outlook on life. They lived in a studio which she rented, and Claude made friends with English children of his own age. In his holidays his mother took him and his sister on long touring holidays, hiring yachts to explore the Greek islands and doing everything possible to wipe out the pain and loss he still felt at his father's rejection. He went to school in Cambridge for a while. It was a school for foreigners where Françoise herself had passed the Higher English examination, and Claude became equally fluent. One of his friends, an Italian girl, later became the wife of Rajiv Gandhi, India's Prime Minister.

'I felt he had to get away from me for a while,' Françoise says. 'After the English school, I sent him to New York. I thought that my not being there with him would make him feel less protected, more able to stand on his own feet and get over his feelings of being cut off from his father.' It might have worked. In some ways Claude did learn to stand on his own feet. He discovered he had a talent for photography, and lived a full and colourful life among the artists and creative New Yorkers who found him and his name equally attractive. But the moods of despair never left him. The little boy who had looked so sweet and happy in his father's portraits became withdrawn and shy, suffering from periods of chronic depression. For three years, in the States, he went into analysis with a New York psychoanalyst. It was during this period that he met Sara. They were married in New York's City Hall on 4 January 1969.

Like all Picasso's children (with the exception of six-foot-tall Paulo), Claude made up in presence and personality for what he lacked in stature. His famous name seemed to confer a sort of grandeur of its own. His lack of height was no bar in Sara's case because she, too, was small, but it was emphasized by his over-long arms which tended to hang awkwardly by his sides. This sight would rouse a protective maternal fondness in her. He was quiet, had pleasant, self-effacing manners, and his striking ebony eyes revealed only his Spanish ancestry rather than his mother's Gallic strain. Women found him attractive. He was soft-voiced and could be amusing and charming, though ultimately Sara found his moods more than she could bear. They had the effect, she says, of altering him so radically that he might not have been the same person. When the first blissful year was over and rows between them began, leading to their separation and divorce after only two years together, she accepted that their differences outweighed the warm feelings she had for him.

The change was fundamental, stemming from a growing awareness of his position in life. At first he had treated his relationship to the world's wealthiest artist as something of a joke, a bizarre accident. 'If I ever inherit his works, I will set up my father's sculptures in New York squares where everyone can enjoy them,' he told Sara. There were amusing escapades in which she took part. 'We came through customs once with some of his father's pictures, and also some by his mother. The officer was suspicious. "What are these?" he asked. "Are they valuable works of art?" "Oh, no," Claude told him, "they're just things my mother and father did." They let him through!'

They took an apartment near the university where Sara was studying, and lived an energetic, comfortable and largely compatible life among the arty Manhattan and Brooklyn crowds. She read his mother's book in secret, because Claude was trying to shield her from the traumas of his early life. A story in it bothered her. 'It described how they, Françoise and Picasso, would paint in different rooms. Claude would not be allowed in either. He'd come to his mother's door and beg to be let in to talk to her. "Go to your father," she'd tell him. Then he'd call out "But you paint better than Daddy!" – and she'd let him in. I was so moved by that story. How lonely he must have been!'

He told her very little at first about those days, but slowly she wore down his reluctance. It was hard to believe that he and his father could have reached such an impasse for such a one-sided reason. Claude and his sister Paloma were utterly without blame in Sara's eyes. If Picasso rejected them, it had to be due to something between Picasso and their mother. Even so, it seemed extraordinarily vengeful and cruel to her.

Claude told Sara, and later his mother, that soon after his father erected the barrier between them he had made a half-hearted attempt to take his own life. Sara remembers 'something about a wall, jumping off a wall'. Françoise confirms that the possibility of suicide had occurred. If it had succeeded, Picasso's escutcheon would have been doubly stained with Claude's and Pablito's blood, but with far greater impact in Claude's case, because it would have occurred during his father's lifetime. Poor Pablito only succeeded in hurting the great man's memory. As a serious French newspaper commented at the time of Pablito's funeral: 'One cannot dismiss the thought that a little more humanity would have prevented a terrible and irreparable act by this young man, so thwarted in his affections.' Claude was also thwarted, his genius and lasting love for his father torn out by the roots. Sara still finds it hard to avoid the belief that he was the victim of extraordinary paternal cruelty which damaged him and helped to destroy their marriage.

Another shadow which blighted Claude's life was his heart condition and the decision he had to take whether or not to undergo surgery to correct it. His mother says: 'There was always an option. At the beginning, I had seen that heart surgery was making tremendous progress so I wanted to wait a while. Then, when he was about eighteen and his doctors recommended it, I thought at that point that he had to make the choice himself. So I left it to him – it was his life, after all. And he elected not to have it.' Had it been done at that time, the chances are that Claude's condition would have been fully cured, she believes. 'But I could not choose for him. A pity, perhaps, because the best time would have been before he was thirty. Now it would be more risky.'

Françoise believes that this worry hung heavily over her son during the weeks and months following his father's death. 'He felt and still feels a kind of fatality hanging over him. For example, now that he has a child [his son, Jasmin, by a second marriage, to American Sydney Russell], he is always asking me what will happen if he dies young. I tell him he probably has no need to worry about that, and to do what he thinks is right. But what it means is that he does worry about it. He feels it weighing on his destiny.'

Physical restrictions imposed by his heart condition hampered any display of natural aggression by Claude. Throughout his early life he had had to report regularly to hospital for lengthy and unpleasant check-ups, involving complex investigations. In some of these a catheter was inserted into his main artery. As his mother says, 'He was made constantly aware of the fact that he was at risk. At one time he thought he would not live.' Nevertheless, when the battle over the inheritance began, he took an active part in it. He was assured that the defect, provided he took care, would not restrict him. According to his mother his physical condition was 'not all that bad'. The stress of carrying a defective heart through life, however, had not been made easier by the rupture with his father. Françoise remembers him telling her about 'a terrible scene with Picasso during that last sad summer visit to Mougins. His father had told him in so many words: You are young, and I am old. I wish you were dead! It left an indelibly damaging impression on him.'

While married to Sara, Claude lived a normal life, enjoying the freedom of New York, mixing with the media and an artistic crowd of various nationalities. His work progressed, and she was doing well in the theatre, winning several comedy roles. One day curiosity made her ask to be taken to meet his father so that she could see for herself what qualities in Picasso had led to his ostracism of Claude. She admits now that she did not fully understand what she was asking. In her young, carefree way Sara believed that the situation would be magically resolved if her father-in-law could meet her and see how happy his son was with her. She might appeal to him, and perhaps help to heal the breach between father and son. This pipe-dream became a subject which they would discuss openly with friends, some of whom shared her view. Françoise blames these friends for what happened. She believes they persuaded Claude to try to use his bride as a hostage to fortune with his estranged father.

Claude finally agreed to approach his half-brother, Paulo, asking him to intercede on his behalf with their father. Sara was delighted. When Paulo came back with the news that if they would come to Mougins he was sure Picasso would see them, she was over the moon. The prospect of a trip to the Côte d'Azur as Madame Picasso became a storybook fantasy to her. The thought of meeting and spending time with the world's greatest living artist was irresistibly exciting. When they flew over and Claude took her to stand on the hillside road at Vauvenargues overlooking his father's sixteenth-century château, announcing in matter-of-fact tones, 'That is my father's castle,' she was overcome. As she later told friends in New York, 'Imagine, a Jewish kid from Brooklyn with a husband whose family own a castle!'

But the visit that started out as a dream soon became a nightmare. They went to keep their appointment with Paulo, but he did not turn up. They sat in a café trying to decide what, if anything, they should do. Claude was inclined to forget the whole thing, to accept Paulo's absence as a further snub from his father. Sara was less sensitive: 'I was impatient and headstrong. I urged: "Come on, Claude, let's go and see him anyway." I couldn't believe it was so difficult. And in the end he agreed.'

They had been married two months. Sara was still overwhelmed by the fact that she was actually married to Picasso's son, even if her mother could not pronounce his name and had never heard of the painter. She desperately wanted to meet the great father-in-law that fate had willed her. The magic of the whole trip depended on it. At noon that day they drove up to the chained gate on the far side of the Mougins moat. It was, she remembers, a slatted five-bar iron affair with rusty barbed wire threaded through it and a rough stone wall extending to either side. Behind lay only a dense tree-covered hillside with no sign of the house beyond. There was a still, almost eerie, atmosphere to the place. The men posted at the gate did nothing to relieve the gloomy impression. Claude stopped the car, got out, and covered the last few yards on foot along a pitted pathway. Sara remembers the scene which followed with disbelief.

'Claude rang a bell, and a security man asked, "Who are you?" He said, "I'm Claude." The man asked again, "Claude who?" though it was perfectly obvious since Claude is very like his father. Claude said, "I'm Claude Picasso. I want to see my father." The man went away. He came back, shaking his head. "He's too busy to see you." Claude – and I greatly admired him for this – said quietly, "Well, can I come back tomorrow?" The man just shook his head again. "No," he said, "I don't think he'll have time tomorrow."

'I looked at Claude. He looked at me. I could see he was terribly upset. Then, as we were standing there not knowing what to do next a truck drew up. Some men – I took them to be plumbers – called out to the security men at the gate and it was opened for them. Claude turned to one of the men in the truck and asked, "Why can't I go in, if you can?" The man laughed. "Oh, you need a passport to get in there," he said. We went away in silence. Neither of us spoke for two hours.'

Since her divorce Sara has remarried and had a baby daughter. She refuses to blame Claude's rejection by his father for the breakdown of their marriage, but during the months that followed the abortive Mougins visit the strain between the young couple noticeably increased. She began to notice an insecurity, 'a terrible dark side' to Claude's nature which she describes as resembling 'a heavy black cloud hanging over his head'. While he could be amusing and light-hearted, and is known in the family as a kind, easygoing man, any minor irritations between them now flared into an open row. At the end they were fighting ferociously, though he was never violent towards her. 'He did most harm to himself. Once, he smashed his fist through a wall of our apartment.'

In one way the marriage had forged a link between Claude and his father which his mother's *conseil de famille* trust enforced. From Picasso's lawyers, a cheque for four hundred dollars was sent to the couple every month. Since it was signed by Picasso, Sara now wishes she had hung on to at least one of them 'for the value of the signature, which would have been worth more than I got out of the marriage!' At the time of their divorce she received a few hundred dollars and almost nothing else. All works by his father that Claude brought into the marriage had to be returned, under the conditions of their marriage contract, and this she concurred with.

Years later, when the inheritance of his father's millions was settled, Sara began to wonder if she had been over-generous. Lawyers advised that there was a perfectly good case for claiming some of the works and possessions brought into their joint possession while married. She had signed a document at the outset, agreeing to forfeit works by his father already in his possession at the time they were married, but surely some had come to them as mutual possessions.

Almost ten years from the day they were married, Sara faced Claude in another court in New York for what was to prove a heartrending and unavailing wrangle over these works. Sara was by then living on what she made in the theatre, while Claude was assured of vast wealth. He used all his newfound power to win the case against his ex-wife. For three snowy, ice-cold days in January 1979 she fought the whole Picasso family and lost. Françoise was in court, looking hostile. Paloma showed none of the friendliness

Sara had received from her earlier. She battled on for what she believed to be her rights, but with only one witness to support her and no battery of expensive lawyers such as Claude could afford to retain.

Sara had already returned all but a tiny silver christening mug and a painting by Luc Simon, his mother's first husband, under the terms of the paper she had signed. In court, Claude looked so stern and businesslike she could hardly believe he was the man she had married. Against her one witness he brought eleven to back up his arguments. Sara was told that she had signed away her right in law to any of his father's works and in fact had no right to anything at all. In a despairing gesture, she took the last few relics of their marriage – the tiny cup given to him by his father and the painting – and in open court offered them back to her ex-husband.

'I walked over and said: "I want to return these like everything else of yours we had." He didn't answer. He just looked at me with incredible intensity. There were all sorts of emotions mirrored in his face, and a lot of anger. I couldn't help it, I cried out: "You hate me so much. Why?"' She has yet to discover the answer to that question. She found, after the divorce and during the abortive court action, that no Picasso would befriend her once she was on the outside. In that way the family showed a remarkable sense of unity.

Sara had known Françoise, Maya and Paloma during her marriage, getting on well with all of them at the time. Though Françoise had regretted the match, she treated her daughter-in-law with warmth and consideration, introducing her to her mother, Claude's grandmother, in Paris and spending time with her. Maya would take her to lunch occasionally, while Paloma was in and out of their life as long as Sara was married to her brother. After the court case, things changed radically. Sara was in Andy Warhol's office one day when Paloma was there. (Andy was a close friend of Paloma.) 'We rode down together in the elevator and she didn't say a single word to me. Just smiled and went off in another direction.'

Claude's ill-health had never been a matter of concern to her during their marriage. 'He didn't seem to worry about it.' But she knew he was supposed to be undergoing psychotherapy and urged him to keep it up when he told her he no longer believed it was doing any good. Paloma, she saw, was the healthier of the two, and Claude seemed almost envious of his sister's physical wellbeing. Paloma's air of vitality was in such total contrast to Claude's morose, changeable behaviour that Sara believed they had experienced very different reactions to their father's rejection. According to their mother, their attitudes to life – with Paloma determined to make her own career while Claude is happy to take a back seat – have largely been influenced by this difference. 'It accentuated the feeling Claude has that she can do things while he cannot. It had, of course, allowed Paloma to be more outgoing, because she felt that she had all that good health and must do something with it.'

Their father's rejection hit them both equally, since they were both teenagers with only two years between them in age. But Paloma's reaction was to carve out her own course in life, refusing to be known only as Picasso's illegitimate daughter, at odds with her father and his second wife. If she was to have none of his millions, then at least she could use the talents he had given her. These were her natural heritage, which nobody could dispute or take away. She is lucky in being ideally fitted for success, with or without a famous name. Slim and fine-boned, Paloma's smallness seems to enhance the contrast of her raven hair and black Spanish eyes with the ivory pallor of her skin. She has perfect taste and has applied it to designing a range of jewellery, latterly lending her name to an exclusive perfume. She has developed a top-executive poise, the air of a woman who knows and expects that doors will be opened for her.

All Paloma's adult life can be seen as a bid to escape the

label 'Picasso's daughter', the love-child he threw aside but never dispossessed. If she can laugh about the connection in public, she is nevertheless hiding deep psychological scars because of it. Basically an extremely shy young woman, the accident of bearing the Picasso name has awoken within her the determination to succeed in her own right as if bent on a self-imposed crusade. She needs success *as Paloma*, not as Picasso's daughter, and she needs it far more desperately and deeply than most people around her realize.

'All of a sudden her father had shut her out of his life and she never understood why,' her mother says. 'Remember, she was the youngest. She was only four, not even five, when I left him. She went to see her father now and then as she grew up, but in fact she was brought up by my husband, Luc Simon, to whom she was greatly attached.' Nevertheless, Paloma retained her love for the father who had shut her out of his life. 'The one thing that protected me', she says, 'is that I knew that he also loved me very much. I think that that is why I am who I am today. Through all that I have been involved with, the best and the worst, that feeling has always been strong.'

Time undoubtedly alters perspective. A year after her father's death Paloma was nursing other feelings. She told writer Nicolas Adam: 'The last holiday I ever spent with my father was Christmas 1963. When I went back at Easter, the lawyer told me: "No, you cannot see him." "Monsieur was out" for ten years . . . the person I loved most in the world.' She qualifies this now with mature reflection and not a little puzzlement. 'I have wonderful memories, but it's also true that he was hard to grow up with. Survival was all-important.' Then, does she feel that there was a cruel side to her father? She pauses to think, a very controlled woman who rarely speaks of Picasso and never lightly. 'It's always the same. When it's happening you really can't stand it. Afterwards, the good is so much more than the bad. That, for me, is so much more a positive thing than the memory of the other side. From the outside everyone always says, "Oh, I would so like to be the daughter of Picasso! It's so wonderful!' And it was . . . I have marvellous memories. But it's also true that it was that, being Picasso's daughter, which made it so much harder for me to become a real person.'

She saw that a woman needed to work, to be able to make her own career and manage to support herself. It came naturally to her that this was what she must do to make a real life for herself. She had passed her '*bac*' (the French equivalent of A-levels) while the French universities were going through the student riots of 1968. Those *événements* made her abandon any thought of an academic career. Instead she studied theatre, which was good for her because it helped to counteract her natural shyness. Later, she took lessons in jewellery-making and helped her mother and her stepfather Luc, by then divorced but still great friends, to make ornaments for the stage settings that Luc was now designing. The work brought her to the design world.

Paloma drew inspiration from her mother's strength in battling with Picasso and Jacqueline. The blame laid on Françoise's book for the split in the family seemed grossly unfair to her. The facts, as she knew them, seemed to exonerate her mother completely. That her father, with Jacqueline's help and support, should have challenged the rights of Claude and herself on the grounds of a mere book seemed highly unlikely. He had lived most of his life, all the years of his universal fame, in a blaze of publicity and appeared often to like it. Unlike her brother, Paloma was ready to fight, when she was old enough to do so, on her own behalf. She was not, perhaps, ready for all that the fight would involve.

7

A LAWYERS' PICNIC

For a while it seemed that only Françoise was fully aware of the tangled legal jungle Picasso had left behind him. 'I had established contact with a number of people through my family and so on, and frankly I knew more members of the bar in Paris than anyone. The general feeling was that I was doing the right thing [in encouraging my children to press their claim] but that as soon as they instituted an action to establish their rights, the opposing lawyers would fight the case in Grasse, or some very provincial little law court, where things were not very up to date.' And since, with the exception of the widow, Paulo was now generally accepted as Picasso's sole heir and was living it up in Paris with his wife and son on his expectations Françoise's efforts to secure a place in Picasso's succession for her children (and Maya, their half-sister) seemed rather belated. Maître Dumas represented Jacqueline. He spoke for her and Paulo in scorning the claims of the 'illegitimates'. It was a time of intense preparation, and in some cases confusion and indecision.

At this time, Claude publicly denied, through an attorney, that he and his sister were either suing for their rights, or contesting the gift of Picasso's collection of other painters' works to the national gallery of France, the Louvre. In doing so he appeared to be withdrawing their challenge to their stepmother and her questionable ability to protect the vast estate. In fact, he and Paloma had no intention of backing out of the succession. The old lawyer, Gaston Bouthoul, whom their mother had originally retained, announced that the courts' permission was sought to 'enable Picasso's children to see part of their inheritance'. Discouragingly, though, Maya's attempt to gain legal recognition for her place in the succession was thrown out of a court in Grasse.

Two major problems faced Claude: the difficulty of monitoring the evaluation of his father's estate while having as yet no official standing in it, and the anxiety he felt in regard to death duties. He and Paloma had requested the appointment of an official administrator, and Pierre Zecri, a notary attached to the Central Civil Tribunal in Paris, was given control over the estate. The man who was to engage in the lengthy and difficult task of valuing the many thousands of works in Picasso's collection was a distinguished Paris art expert, Maurice Rheims. The French tax system allowed great estates, such as Picasso's, to pay the swingeing twenty or more per cent death duties in works of art – provided these were individually acceptable. It was Zecri and Rheims' duty to see that the state received full value. Their close supervision of the estate made it difficult for anyone else to estimate the true value of 'Picasso's Picassos' irrespective of who would get what.

Possession being nine points of the law, Jacqueline held the whip hand. She supplied an inventory of what she believed the extent of the works to be. Claude was shown it. 'It was a joke,' he says. 'The whole thing was only a hundred and twenty pages or so long. Of course I didn't accept that. And on the taxation issues, she wanted to make

over ninety per cent of the works! A very generous lady!' It
had been jointly agreed that the death duties' bill would be
met by *dation*, but Claude pressed for and was able to
arrange for his own experts to examine the collection. 'We
came up with 75,000 entries. Our inventory was three
metres long! To establish just the basic facts took more than
three years, and we still had to work out an equitable
distribution.'

The professionals crowded round like flies to a honeypot.
On one day in Pierre Zecri's office, five of the possible heirs
found themselves seated at a huge table encompassed by
no less than seventeen dark-suited, smiling gentlemen. None
of the Picassos present looked as happy. Eight were lawyers,
six were listed as 'financial advisers'. Then there was the
official art appraiser Maurice Rheims, one unspecified eld-
erly gentleman wearing dark glasses, and legal administ-
trator Pierre Zecri himself. If the professionals' attendance
fees for that one meeting had been added up they would
have amounted to more than Picasso, who often paid for
meals in kind by drawing on a restaurant tablecloth, earned
in a whole year during his early life. Both Zecri and Rheims
were carrying out lengthy, if essential, researches at the cost
of the state. The administrator was charging half of one per
cent of the notarized value of Picasso's entire inheritance
as his fee.

As well as this the knowledge that more than a fifth of
the entire inheritance would be forfeit to meet the tax bill
became steadily more galling as valuation went on. France's
cultural minister, André Malraux, had first proposed the
dation system of payment of *doits de mort* some years before.
His suggestion had passed into law at the end of 1968 while
Picasso was still alive. If it had prompted the artist's gift to
the nation – his collection of paintings by others – in the
hope of being excused part of this hefty levy on his personal
estate, the gambit did not pay off. The Act left selection in
state hands, with no guarantee that any offering would
necessarily be accepted. It was within the state's discretion

to say which work would be required, and at what value. The slow, painful valuation now being undertaken in Paris by Rheims in his sunny studio-office in the Faubourg St-Honoré was crucial. But how long would it take and what would the total result be?

Rheims faced a task which today he dismisses with dry humour as 'near impossible'. Describing it, he gestures out of the full-length window in his office at an autumnal scene, the wind blowing the leaves from the trees and sending them eddying down the street. 'To value Picasso's works is like forecasting what the wind will bring. Who knows what Picasso's value will be with the passage of time?' In addition to the frightening costs involved, there was a suspicion in the family that perhaps everything was not being administered as scrupulously as it might have been. Claude says there was 'much dirty work . . . some people did not act very ethically'. Marina was reportedly accusing Jacqueline of salting away some of the paintings and other works of art, and some of the hoarded money, in Switzerland. She now disclaims this but admits that 'the general feeling in the family was that lots of things were disappearing. We didn't go to court about it – that was journalists' stuff. But we did raise it with her.'

Marina also challenged the fees which the estate was having to pay Zecri and others. She was now filling in time between meetings and disputes with creative work – making pottery – for which she had inherited some of her grandfather's talent. Above all, her harsh early life and experiences had taught her the value of money. 'Mr Zecri was always pleasant to me,' she says, 'but he made such a terrific lot of money. So, too, did Mr Rheims. They took *milliards* of francs for their services, and I really thought it was too much.'

She was by no means alone in this. Françoise laughs now at what she agrees was 'a lawyers' picnic' lasting the full five years and more of the tussle over the succession. Her own previous involvement with the law on her children's behalf had been a testing experience which few women in her position – comfortably married to a world-famous scientist – would have persisted in. 'But as I said when Jacqueline refused to allow my children to attend their father's funeral, it was her influence that had been responsible for Picasso's hideously unjust rejection of them for ten years. I was determined they should have legal redress.' The lawyer she had used in the earlier action, Maître Bouthoul, was now an old man. His cautious advice was no longer what they wanted. They needed someone closer to the changing pattern of French law. And someone they could trust. 'In the lower courts like the one at Grasse, it was always possible, I believed, that the clerk or one of the officers could be swayed by loyalty to Picasso.'

Françoise had one stroke of luck before Picasso died. Maître Izard, a distinguished advocate who was one of Picasso's lawyers in the case he lost against the publishers of her book, suddenly offered his services. Françoise was surprised to get a call from him suggesting a meeting to which she should bring Claude and Paloma. 'Bizarre! My first thought was that it was another trick, a way to betray me. And asking me to bring the children to the meeting seemed a bit much! Anyway, I went.'

But could she rely on him? Experience had taught Françoise that waging a fight against Picasso or his widow was not, as her son Claude would have put it, 'a cricket tea party'. In any bid to secure their own ends both Pablo and Jacqueline were devious fighters who would use whatever weapons came to hand. Izard might, she thought, be their secret weapon. 'The lawyer began by assuring me that he was "not my enemy". But I had made up my mind that I wouldn't be nice to him, or trust him, until I was very sure of his intentions. So I simply told him, "No, and I'm not yours – since you lost your case against me."

'He took it rather well. "Well, anyway, let's be friends now," he said. "Let's forget all about that." I told him, "OK, we'll forget it. But I do not think you can take my children's case now, having once been against me. You can't switch from one side to the other; it is a conflict of interests." Maître Izard disagreed. "But I can," he said. "Don't forget that Picasso's lawsuit over the book was not against you but against Calman Levy, your publishers. Of course I can take your children's case." That was marvellous. What a bit of luck!' The wrangling over the book had brought her a lawyer who admired her determination, who had worked for and understood her vengeful lover, and who wanted above all to secure the rights of her children.

Sadly, Izard's participation was short-lived. Six months after their meeting he suffered a heart attack and died. Françoise had no choice but to accept this loss philosophically and to look for a replacement, but the alliance had been useful. 'It was still wonderful that he had joined us. And the fact that *he* had made that move, that he had switched sides, proved very important psychologically.'

Nevertheless, Izard's death caused six months' delay in Claude and Paloma's action to establish their rights under the new Act. Meanwhile, Françoise was hard put to find someone to replace him. 'I didn't want somebody else who would die on the job. I had to find somebody younger, a really good jurist who had had time to study everything in the case and would take all necessary action with all possible speed. I went to see two or three who were not quite right. Then I found the ideal man.' Friends had recommended Jean-Denis Bredin. He was a lawyer whose knowledge of jurisprudence was exceptionally well suited to the intricacies of the case. 'He was exactly what we needed. I chose him at once. Or, to put it more accurately, I advised my children to take him and they did. It was a good move. Bredin could not be bought, which was the most important thing of all.' By then, she was moving between the South of France and California to help conduct the campaign, with the full support of her husband, Jonas Salk.

Françoise would much have preferred to be the one in

the firing line, but the children were legally of age and the action had to be in their names. In the hope of avoiding a long round of legal haggling, she went to see Paulo. The meeting was not a success. 'I told Paulo to exercise his rights as Picasso's son and heir. There was a lawyer called de Sariac, who was one of the trustees in our *conseil de famille* and was also advising Jacqueline. I told Paulo to seek his advice.' She must have hoped in advising him to do so that she would bring Paulo to her side of the battle. He should go to the lawyer, she urged, and insist that all papers and documents in the case be handed over to him as principal heir rather than to Jacqueline. With de Sariac already associated with her and the children in the *conseil*, this would have been greatly to their advantage. It was a cunning move, but it failed. 'Paulo, so soon after his father's death, was not very clever. He didn't follow what I was telling him. And the entanglements were too much for his poor brain to grasp.'

Françoise and the children left the meeting with little hope that Paulo would support their claims. She had failed to impress on him the threat of what long wrangling would do to the succession or how seriously a 'conflict of interest' could delay and possibly neutralize settlement for them all. Paulo was left in no doubt that the lines of battle were drawn – that, with Maître Bredin's skills to guide them, Françoise and the children were ready for any engagement – but Jacqueline's influence over him was already too strong to allow him to back down.

Nevertheless, Françoise managed to gain one valuable advantage from the meeting. By encouraging Paulo to show sympathy to Claude and Paloma, his half-brother and -sister, she persuaded him to let them have right of access to the Picasso archives. 'That was vital, because it enabled us to know what was and what was not in the estate.' She also tried to secure the same easy passage for Maya, their half-sister. 'She lived in the South of France with her husband and their three children. I thought it would be much better if she had her own lawyer and this was arranged. So, you see, all this isolated Jacqueline a great deal. It put everything into the lawyers' hands on both sides. Which, of course, added to the fruits of the "lawyers' picnic" but was otherwise exactly what I wanted.'

In March 1974, Claude and Paloma won the right to set aside all previous obstacles and objections to their birthright, despite Maître Dumas' opposition. Maya was equally successful shortly afterwards. From spring 1974, therefore, there were five legally accepted heirs.

Then, suddenly and unexpectedly, Paulo died on 6 June 1975. His death – more from exhaustion than from anything else, it would seem – introduced two more claimants, his heirs. More important still, it brought in their mothers. If Paulo had been English or American, his widow Christine would have enjoyed the same rights of inheritance as he had in his lifetime. In France the law is different. There everything passes to the children, which, in Paulo's case, meant that both Bernard, his son by Christine, and Marina, his daughter by Emilienne, the ex-wife he openly detested, would inherit equally. Paulo's two widows, Emilienne and Christine, were as determined as Françoise to see that their children received their rightful portion of the estate. They entered the battle of the succession with one great advantage: their children were Picasso's *legitimate* grandchildren. Whatever the new Act might do to accommodate *enfants adulterins*, the newcomers would take precedence. There were, therefore, six heirs. The complexities of the settlement were increasing rather than diminishing. Accepting that they must all get something, who was to decide the proportions in which the disposition of the estate should be made?

In one sense Paulo was well out of the battle. He had not been trained or equipped to deal with legal complexities or the administration of great wealth. If he had lived, the wrangles and squabbles of his divided family would have shown him up even further as the inadequate, ineffectual man he was, emphasizing his failure to come anywhere near his famous father in intellect or accomplishment. To that extent Paulo's death removed one complication, but others ensued from it.

Marina was back from a brief stay in England, and difficulties were arising between herself and her mother. The sudden change in her position would in time make it possible for her to give her mother all that Emilienne craved. Marina understood and would honour her duty in this respect, but her immediate desire was to set up a home for handicapped children, an ambition she had nursed since the days when she had worked in such a home. First, though, she and her half-brother Bernard must succeed to their father's role in the settlement, that of principal legitimate heirs to a vast and complicated estate. Marina had long been conscious of Jacqueline's influence over her grandfather. Now it became a matter of personal pride not to allow herself to be dominated by the widow.

Marina was twenty-four, Bernard not yet sixteen. With their father's death, they had succeeded to the principal position in the succession. Whatever happened to Maya, Claude and Paloma's claims, legitimate grandchildren would share the greater portion with Jacqueline. The question was how the division would be made.

The night before her father died, Marina had dreamed that he was falling into an abyss. Paulo was holding out his arms towards her, warning her about her coming fortune. Nothing she could do in the dream could prevent the catastrophe of his death or the threat posed by her looming fortune. When she awoke to the news that she was now one of the main heirs in line of descent, the realization of her changed position came as a terrible shock. Her father's warning hung over her still. In newspaper stories she was being referred to as 'the richest heiress in the world'. Within weeks she was caught up in the legal tangle, closeted for hours with lawyers, locked in endless discussions with the other heirs to decide how, when and by what means they might split the immense fortune to everyone's benefit and satisfaction.

Marina and Bernard immediately inherited a half-share each in the annual allowance which Paulo had been paid by his father, now disbursed by the estate's administrators. The days of penury in the small house in Golfe-Juan were receding fast for Marina, but a full understanding of what the inheritance and its attendant battles would mean to her was slow in coming. She had known so little of her grandfather. Jacqueline, she felt, was the cause of that. Her protection of Picasso had reduced his relationship with his family to almost nil. Furthermore, it had set her father apart from her. Yet now she had to meet Jacqueline as an equal.

Four days after her father's death Marina nerved herself for the first encounter. All six heirs had agreed to meet in the chambers of official administrator Pierre Zecri in Paris, to hammer out at least the rudiments of an agreement in principle. It was an anticlimax, because Jacqueline did not come, pleading ill-health which would not permit her to make the journey. Another reason may have been that she saw no advantage in being part of a gathering which would almost certainly seek to reduce her control over Picasso's fortune, and perhaps reduce her portion of it. The fact that the 'others' were now exercising legitimate rights in the succession may also have made her feel less than well.

Without the widow's presence the meeting was inconclusive. Marina and the others were left with no clear idea of their future inheritances, or of how the settlement – the sharing out of the enormous hoard of paintings, sculptures, engravings, drawings and ceramics left by Picasso in his various homes and banks – would be made. The impression left was of lawyers and advisers leading the disputing family into a legal maze of escalating costs which, in the end, might swallow up nearly all the inheritance. In the heirs' opinion the whole unwieldly process of the law seemed to be advancing in slower and infinitely more costly measure than the proverbial mills of God. With Jacqueline refusing to deal

with the others directly, the succession was becoming a
fragmented struggle in which the family, the six heirs and
those associated with them – such as Maya's mother Marie-
Thérèse, Bernard's mother Christine, Marina's mother
Emilienne, and Claude and Paloma's mother Françoise –
ranged themselves in 'clans', each suspicious of the other.

One clan was led by Marina and her teenage half-brother,
Bernard. His mother, Christine, was a helpful ally, but
Emilienne was still emotionally unbalanced by the shock of
her son's suicide, still nursing grievances against the dead
Paulo and his father for their part in Pablito's death and
her years of relative poverty. Marina could not look to her
for counsel and support.

Jacqueline was a clan on her own. Claude told the American writer Carolyn Paul of *ARTnews* that his stepmother
continued to fight against their inclusion in the succession,
even though he and Paloma had won full rights in law to
do so. 'At one point when she refused to sign some papers
we threatened to take her to court. When she found out
that the law was on our side and that she would not only
lose her case but have to pass us damages for the loss of
interest to the estate, she sure signed quickly enough.'
Claude had found that guerrilla tactics were often necessary
to beat off raids by the rival clans. In the same interview
with Carolyn Paul, published in the summer of 1978, he
revealed that there had been a falling out with Marina. 'She
felt slighted by the fact that [under the proposed settlement]
some of the properties were being given to her half-brother
Bernard. . . . We threatened to take her to court, too, with
the same result. She dropped it when she found out how
much it would cost her.' On the other hand he confirmed
that the family had clubbed together to provide Marina
with 'a gift' in the form of an advance. She was now sharing
the position of first in line to the succession, yet her means
remained modest.

By December 1976 the family disputes had become so
hopelessly unresolved, so seemingly endless, that a court

hearing was arranged at which the heirs would *have* to come together, Jacqueline included, or forfeit their rights. Once more the lawyers on all sides rubbed their hands in expectation of further juicy fees, but the hearing never came about. It was cancelled by common consent when at the last minute Jacqueline announced that she was ready to sign what everyone else had signed. If she had meant it, *l'affaire Picasso* would have been settled in half an hour, and only four years after Picasso's death. But, as before, she had a change of heart. Both she and Marina continued to challenge a number of small points in the proposed settlement with the determination of fox terriers. Marina's legal counsel, Guy Ferreboeuf, explained that 'highly complicated illegalities' existed in the agreement as drawn up by the others which had to be ironed out.

The state of mind of the heirs at this time was not helped by these niggling, often secretive manoeuvrings. Paloma seemed the least disturbed by them. Her commercial life, launching the jewellery she had designed herself, was given wide publicity in the world's press, and her beauty added an element of newsworthy glamour to the press's occasional coverage of the mysterious goings-on in the settlement of her father's fortune.

She had also appeared nude in a film, *Immoral Tales*, to the scandalmongers' delight. Photographs of her small, exquisite body were featured in magazines and on television. The efforts she was making to realize a full career for herself as Paloma, rather than as Picasso's daughter, were discussed in many interviews. The film was made partly in Sweden and partly in France by a Polish director. In it, Paloma played a bloodthirsty seventeenth-century Hungarian countess. One scene showed her naked in bed with another girl. Asked by an interviewer if this had embarrassed her, or whether the family would find it embarrassing, Paloma said: 'I don't see why. They've seen me walking around the house naked.' She had 'experimented' with the film part, she said, but had no wish to go on with an acting career. There were other areas she preferred, such as designing jewellery. (And, subsequently, the creation of a delicious scent, given her own name.) Alongside all this, she was helping to catalogue her father's works.

Paloma was a busy lady. She travelled widely in Europe and the United States. In New York she designed fur coats; in Italy sheets, linen and crystal ornaments. The jewels she made up into stylized patterns – more for display than for adornment – in Greece. She was, as she said, 'always travelling'.

One very important consideration for Paloma and her brother was the protection and perpetuation of Picasso's name. The idea of a museum to house the state's *dation* was already being discussed. Much thought was going into the form it would take, the need for a key person from the art world to run it, and the site of a suitably distinguished building to house it. Once more Jacqueline had her own ideas. She declared through her lawyers that she would make Vauvenargues, Picasso's burial place, both a museum and a shrine to her beloved husband's memory. Told that the state had other ideas, that Paris would be given the honour of displaying for posterity the magnificent works preserved among those of 'Picasso's Picassos' which would fall into the state's hands when the *dation* had been agreed, she let it be known that *her* exhibition would nevertheless proceed. It has since travelled to many cities and towns in and out of France and includes the finest of the works which remain in her possession.

Selection of the beautiful ruined Hôtel Salé in Paris to house the Musée Picasso (where the taxed *dation* pictures and sculptures would be on permanent display) came later. Claude might have seemed an ideal choice to be its director and would no doubt have accepted the post with delight, but it was felt that it would be preferable to appoint an experienced curator with expert knowledge of Picasso's works. Dominique Bozo, the man finally appointed, fulfilled both requirements.

Claude, anyway, had more than enough on his hands at this time. Paloma later explained to her friend Lester Persky, the Hollywood producer: 'It was like the days with my father when we felt we were living with Brigitte Bardot. If it wasn't the press, it was the people. We had a mob around us most of the time.' She was pleased that their legal right to be included in the succession had now been settled, but not surprised. 'At least the law was better now. We were getting half as much as the legitimate heirs, which was something. But the idea of an adulterous child not being as good as a legitimate child seemed to me absurd, sort of bourgeois. It harks back to the old thing of despising bastards, which always seemed funny to me. If anyone had called me a bastard, it would have made me laugh.'

The effect of the delay on the others, less involved in the work of selection, cataloguing and administration, was of aggrieved impatience with the slow process of the law. Not unnaturally they wanted their money, but first it would be good to know how much they might expect, and Rheims still had not completed his valuation. Occasionally the frustrating delay proved unbearable. Bernard, now in his late teens, was the first to be affected by it. 'He stopped being the nice, quiet boy we had known,' an artist friend explains. 'He became very nervous, very shy of everyone. And what the French call *branché* [literally 'switched on'], with a love of parties and friends who shared his taste for good restaurants and other forms of high living.'

Maya continued as best she could to bring up her children in Marseilles and to look after her marine engineer husband, Pierre Widmaier. Her mother was fast becoming a problem which worried her deeply. Marie-Thérèse was sickening, her life blighted by Picasso's death and the obsessional belief that theirs had been the only true love of his life. For her, the days passed slowly. There was so much sadness, so many tragedies. Her beloved lay in his grave unable to receive or reply to the long letters in which she had always confided to him her hopes and fears. With his passing a light had gone out of her life, and now she viewed the squabbles of the heirs – including her own daughter – with mournful bewilderment. What did it all mean? How could her beloved have caused such terrible things as Pablito's suicide to happen? The manner of the young man's death – she looked upon him as virtually her step-grandson – preyed on her fuddled mind. Why had he been driven to such an action? Why should such horrors have been heaped on the descendants of such a man as Picasso? Marie-Thérèse stood only on the fringe of the family and its disputes, but her influence on them was soon to be considerable.

8

SETTLEMENT

Bernard was still not of legal age, eighteen, so Christine as his legal administrator had to speak for him in the settlement negotiations. With the history of bad blood between Paulo's two families, this placed Marina in an awkward situation. She settled it, she says, by making a generous present to her stepmother, though nothing like the 'million pounds' quoted in press reports, which talked falsely of Christine being 'bought out'. Marina acted only after consultation with Claude, Paloma and Maya. 'We agreed I should offer her some works of art and listed them. The arrangement was that she should have them only in her lifetime.'

Altogether, Marina's handling of the inheritance now bound to come to her seems to have been sensible. The young woman who had tragically lost a brother, who had bitterly accused her father and grandfather of meanness and cruelty, was now a person of consequence in her own right. She stood on the same footing as her half-brother Bernard and ranked, in law, ahead of Picasso's widow Jacqueline in the succession. As to her aunts and uncle, Maya, Paloma and Claude, they would jointly receive no more than her single share. An element of luck also favoured her. When Pablito shocked the world with his horrendous suicide, the news of it brought great distress to the woman who was virtually Marina's step-grandmother, Marie-Thérèse Walter. Picasso's adoring mistress had struck up a friendship with Emilienne Picasso, so was close to Marina and her mother during the months leading up to Pablito's death. She was consequently anxious to do whatever she could to help Marina in her new role as a leading inheritor of Picasso's vast wealth.

Fortunately, Marie-Thérèse had some experience of the art world. When Picasso's affair with Dora Maar drove her away from him, Marie-Thérèse had taken with her a number of her lover's canvases which she believed herself entitled to. Through a dealer who knew her, Marie-Thérèse later tried to sell some of the works. Her friend put her in touch with another dealer, a man called Bergrine, to whom she offered the paintings. Bergrine apparently doubted her right to ownership and contacted Picasso, whose lawyers became involved. Ultimately Picasso had allowed Marie-Thérèse to keep the pictures on the understanding that she would not sell them in his lifetime.

Thus, with Picasso's death, Marie-Thérèse was able to release a number of early Picassos on to the art market. Soon afterwards, a young Dutchman who had become friendly with Marie-Thérèse (by now she was surrounding herself with young men in a pathetic attempt to recapture the days of her youth and beauty) told a dealer in Holland about the Picassos he had seen in her home, and with which she was willing to part. The Dutch dealer telephoned a London friend who was both a Picasso expert and an international dealer and gave him Marie-Thérèse's telephone number. A few days later the London expert flew to the South of France where he was met by Marina and taken to see Marie-Thérèse. She told him that she was deeply sorry for Marina and her mother, Emilienne, whose small maintenance payments had been stopped by Jacqueline as soon as Picasso died, and that she wanted to set up a trust in Marina's favour after she had sold the paintings.

The Englishman knew that a Swiss dealer, Jan Krugier, was staying in his wife's family home nearby. He put them in touch and personally introduced Marie-Thérèse to Krugier, with highly beneficial results. When Marina, on her father's death, learned that she was about to inherit an artistic fortune of which she had little or no knowledge, she asked Marie-Thérèse to help her and was given Krugier's name as a reliable expert.

Though fully aware of the opportunities offered by the imminent succession, the dealer had made no approach thus far to any member of the family. A diffident man, Krugier disliked the idea of putting himself forward when, as he says, 'the whole art world was on the scent'. Even his wife's encouragement (she insisted 'you are not a hyena!') had no effect. As he says: 'Marina Picasso, now that her father was dead, was to inherit one of the largest fortunes in her grandfather's paintings and works of art that the world had ever known. Of course I saw what was involved in the selection, but I also knew that she was certain to have received many approaches. There would be no shortage of dealers and experts she could turn to. What could I do?' In fact, he did nothing. The way his involvement came about was curious.

In August 1976, Jan Krugier was in Venice with his wife, an experienced astrologer, enjoying a pleasant holiday. Madame Krugier became convinced, through planetary observation, that something important was about to happen to her husband. They must return at once, she told him, to her parents' château in southern France. He was enjoying himself, and their holiday still had several days to run. He wanted to stay on. She, however, was insistent and pressed him to follow her advice. Fortunately Krugier places great faith in his wife's predictions. He allowed himself to be persuaded. As he says now, 'It was as well that I did because I really did not want to leave. We had been having a most amusing time in Venice. But Marianne, my wife, has extraordinary gifts and I had to give way to her in the end.'

They arrived in France to be met by Marianne Krugier's father, Prince Poniatowski. 'A lady has been calling you repeatedly,' he told Jan Krugier. 'I think, though I am not sure, her name was Picasso.' It was Marina. She knew now that she was going to inherit, with her half-brother, Bernard, one of the largest shares of the vast estate left by her grandfather. She who had been so poor would be among the world's richest women. Much depended, though, on ensuring that the works which would come into her possession as soon as Rheims' valuation – now nearing completion – was finished were expertly chosen. Several times she had tried to make contact with Jan Krugier, but his number had been changed. It was only when she learned that he might be staying with his father-in-law that she had tried to reach him there and, thanks to his wife's prescience, managed to do so.

When he returned her call Marina told him: 'Look, I need your help. I am going to be very rich, I'm sure you know that. But I really don't know enough about my grandfather's works of art to make the best choice if it is offered to me. I want you to help me do that.' It was not easy for Krugier to accept. In other circumstances he would have been overjoyed to undertake the commission. 'But he knew that it was going to be rough going all the way,' Marianne says. 'If Jan accepted the challenge he would be involved in very difficult areas, some of which were most jealously guarded.' In the end Marina's frank request proved irresistible. 'I told her I would do all I could for her, knowing of course that the task was enormous. The whole art world would be watching the selection.'

Krugier had not overestimated the problems. The works were closely guarded, making even his privileged access to them on Marina's behalf fraught with difficulty and suspicion. As he says now: 'It was really absurdly hard to get anywhere near the works while Zecri had them under his control. I had to use all my powers of persuasion to give her any help at all.' Marina was grateful for what he did for her. 'I needed an agent, somebody who could understand and deal with the commercial world of painting. It is a very special world and there's a big gulf between the painter and somebody who buys and sells paintings. Mr Krugier was an excellent transactor who knew that world perfectly.' The London dealer who, indirectly, had introduced them agrees. 'She was fortunate in finding an expert who knew the value of the works, so that when it came to the selection he picked the best. Marina did very well, believe me, by following Krugier's advice. She had the best Picassos of all the heirs.'

But elsewhere the clamp of official control had closed round the estate. Pierre Zecri carried formidable powers. He and his department were aware of the inevitability of conflict and controversy when it came to the sharing out of the immensely valuable works of art. Some would hold strong sentimental value for a particular heir; others would by virtue of their exceptional artistic merit be worth several times as much as works comparable in size and style and period. Picasso's cubist masterpiece, *Les Demoiselles d'Avignon*, for instance, then in the possession of the New York Museum of Modern Art, was conservatively valued at $35 million. Other works were worth far less, and it was Zecri's duty to see that his choice of 'Picasso's Picassos' for the *dation* did not fall below the value required in death duties.

Despite much guesswork in the press, nobody other than Jacqueline and the officials had a clear idea of the estate's contents, and Jacqueline's knowledge of the works it contained seemed to be restricted to the list she had prepared which Claude had found so inadequate. The sheer size and variety of the collection locked away in various bank strongrooms made it impossible to estimate its worth with any degree of accuracy, and to add to the unknown quantity of their future wealth the heirs had to contend with another uncertainty. Would Jacqueline ever agree to a plan for distributing the works and the properties?

In all their interests, it was crucial that the state should not get more than its fair share. But more and more lawyers were becoming involved, and Claude particularly was alive to the dangers inherent in the 'picnic'. 'Lawyers are mercenary people and some did not, it's true, behave very well. But in an out-and-out battle, which this had become, one has to expect casualties. We hired guns too, you know.'

The question was how much each of the six heirs would be entitled to, and in what proportion to each other, once the state had removed its fifth in value of the whole. While the lawyers dithered, adding hourly to their soaring costs, and the heirs were reported to be squabbling and disputing, Rheims had still not put a value on the whole estate. As to the way the huge cake would be cut, Jacqueline, it was believed, would get a quarter of everything. As the widow and next of kin she would also be allowed (under the same French policy of *usufruit* as Marina's settlement with Christine) a further quarter in her lifetime, provided that this was afterwards surrendered to the descendants, or their descendants. Then the legitimate grandchildren, Marina and Bernard, would stand to gain a third quarter divided equally between them. The final quarter would go to the *adulterins* split three ways between Maya, Claude and Paloma.

All this was conjecture, the gossip of the man in the Paris street. It overlooked the intricacies of French law under which a descendant heir or widow might only benefit from the wealth acquired *during the period of his or her relationship with the deceased*. If press and public were baffled, so, too, were the family. Rheims' deliberation over the valuation was agonizingly slow. In spite of all the documentary evidence, Maya says that it took five years to complete the valuation. It obviously seemed to do so to her. Until it was completed there was no way to assess what number of millions each heir might hope to receive.

Another delicate question which nobody seemed able to hazard more than a guess at was how much cash lay in the locked rooms and caches where Picasso had hidden it. Jacqueline had lost control of these. The overflowing drawers and secret hiding places were now in Zecri's care, and he was officially bound to secrecy. Again, only guesses could be made.

If enough cash had existed to pay off the death duties, that would have settled the matter. As it was, the settlement had to be made in works of art. The final selection would require the heirs' unanimous approval, which, with Jacqueline refusing even to attend meetings or to let her team of lawyers and advisers agree to anything without her full approval and consent, seemed an impossibility. Maurice Rheims made a photographic dossier of 'Picasso's Picassos' numbering no less than 1,885 paintings, 7,089 drawings, 1,228 sculptures and 2,880 ceramics. All these works Picasso had hoarded, or recovered, during his lifetime. Their most gratifying feature was that each of his 'periods' was well represented, as he had obviously intended.

Writing in the authoritative French journal *Le Point* on 11 July 1977, the late Hélène Demoriane added to and expounded on this early list. She asserted that the paintings, tapestries, carpets, illustrated books and other works of art in the estate were then worth over 800 million francs. The drawings would add another 150 million. An additional 4,659 drawings and sketches in 149 notebooks (some now on display at the Musée Picasso in Paris) were worth close to an additional 40 million francs, she disclosed. With 18,095 engravings by Picasso himself, 6,112 lithographs, 3,181 linocuts, 1,353 sculptures and the nearly 3,000 ceramic works, Demoriane estimated the total value at a billion and a quarter francs or, at the then rate of exchange, £175 million. Her article was illustrated by a bored-looking photograph of Claude gazing at a pile of pages as high as his desk, the 'dossiers of the inventory'. The photograph brought home the magnitude of the task he was facing in

trying to participate in the detailed cataloguing and valuation of his father's treasure trove.

At the same time France's Minister of Culture, Michel
Guy, announced his decision to create a Picasso museum
in the seventeenth-century mansion known as the Hôtel
Salé ten minutes' walk from the Pompidou Centre in Paris.
On 21 July 1976, Dominique Bozo, formerly the young
and popular curator of the Musée d'Art Moderne, was
appointed its director. Assisting him was an ex-director of
the same gallery, Jean Leymairie, currently curator of the
Villa Medici in Rome. Bozo's title was to be *maître d'œuvre*,
which meant that he was additionally responsible for planning and carrying out the work on the museum building
itself, which involved a complete renovation and restoration
of the ancient building.

On a pleasant summer's day in Paris, Bozo, a gently
smiling man with glasses and neat greying hair, was shown
Rheims' dossier of photographs. The new director was
overwhelmed. He had already inspected the site of the
proposed museum. It was undoubtedly magnificent but the
dilapidation of its façade, the crumbling grandeur of its vast
rooms and the decrepit condition of the cellars which were
to form part of the necessary floor space – they have since
become a well-lit and spacious crypt – daunted him at first.
It had initially been hoped that work on the project would
be completed in time for the centenary of Picasso's birth in
1981, but the fact that it overran that date by nearly four
years is not surprising. A comparison of photographs of the
unrestored hotel with the splendid gallery it has become
today under Bozo's guiding hand reveals that France and
all lovers of Picasso's art have benefited greatly from the
delay.

Between them, Bozo and Leymairie were to select for the
state the works which would comprise the *dation*. The list
was to be submitted to the family and to a panel of experts,
comprising the late Sir Roland Penrose, Maurice Besset of
Grenoble, and Pierre Daix, a writer. The unknown factor

was how long it would take to get the family to agree to the choice of works for the *dation*. Individually the heirs were reconciled to accepting the state's requirement of 20 per cent of the estate's total value, but they expressed conflicting views and opinions on how this should be met. Claude believed 'not one of us could agree on anything that was happening'. The family were as disunited in wealth as they had been without it.

Against this background the battle for the disputed millions entered its final phase. More than three years had passed since Picasso's death. Maurice Rheims had at last completed his valuation of just under 50,000 separate works. Dominique Bozo had come to terms with all but Jacqueline over the *dation*. The world, especially the French nation, was waiting impatiently to see the astonishing private collection of 'Picasso's Picassos'. Yet nobody except the army of professional lawyers, accountants, financial consultants, tax experts and officials had so far seen more than small advances from the estate. It was known to be worth (for tax purposes, hence probably very much more) £175 million. This was made up of cash (almost exhausted by costs, Marina says), properties (some of these subject to 'trade off' deals between the heirs) and works of art. And Jacqueline, whose signature was needed on every document before settlement could be made, was still failing to attend meetings.

Reports appeared of a 'slanging match' between Marina and Jacqueline (now described by Marina as 'media nonsense'). But the family as a whole were becoming irritated and hostile towards the widow. While they were doing all they could to arrange matters amicably and fairly between them, she seemed to be holding up everything by constant evasions and prevarications. Marina saw her stepgrandmother as the chief obstacle to settlement of a number of points, both on the *dation* and on the succession as a whole. 'She was so often against the agreements we had reached. In the end we found that the best way – the only way – we could reach her was through Maître Dumas. We would agree among ourselves, then present the decision to him to convey to her. That at least made things easier.'

Until the *dation* was decided, nothing else could be done. But the disputed millions were under constant consideration. The clans watched one another for any sign of unfair advantage, sought or gained. If the question was no longer *who* would inherit, its place had been taken by an even greater enigma: how many, and *which*, of the works would each heir get?

Fortunately, as he says, Dominique Bozo was not representing the family. He and his panel of advisers stood outside the wrangling. His job was to select those of the works which, without overstepping the permitted percentage, could most faithfully form a representative collection of the great master's life work in all its many styles and stages. Bozo's Musée Picasso wished to stand aloof from any greedy family grubbings or petty squabbles, but his work was daily becoming more difficult. Not that ministry officials put obstacles in his way, or that Claude's insistence on handling the archives and administration details hindered him. The Paris bank vaults were open whenever he wished to inspect the great horde of treasures stacked within them. Physically, though, the task of selecting works, of seeing and valuing each with his own eyes, was enormously tiring. The restoration of the ancient and beautiful Hôtel Salé was also a slow and demanding business. It was made no easier by the family. Where suspicion and distrust had been kept under wraps during the early disputes, now they were escalating by the day. An analogy to Robert Louis Stevenson's *Treasure Island*, with Picasso's fortune lying like buried treasure under the pirates' feet, is not too far-fetched.

In this climate the press and media could hardly be blamed for making the utmost of the situation, reporting every scrap of gossip and scandal. Marina had 'demanded the dismissal' of Pierre Zecri from his post as official administrator, claiming that his fees – approaching the equivalent of £3 million – were outrageous and exorbitant. She was 'reliably reported' to have accused her stepmother of accumulating money and pictures in Switzerland. This report added that a tribunal at Grasse had thrown out Marina's case as 'inadmissible'. Nevertheless, on her behalf, Jan Krugier studied the trial proceedings and managed to obtain a useful insight into the size of the collection at stake. A list was given in evidence of 1,884 paintings, 7,089 drawings, 1,218 sculptures, 3,222 ceramic works, 11 tapestries, 8 carpets and some £5 million worth of lithographs and engravings. This was proved to be inaccurate later but it was at least a guide. Marina promptly announced from Switzerland, where she was conferring with Krugier, that she would appeal to a higher court in Paris. None of the heirs trusted the local and minor courts where Picasso's influence (and now Jacqueline's) extended insidiously.

Stories were circulating about Jacqueline, too. In Mougins and Vauvenargues the locals were whispering that she had suffered some sort of collapse from grief. She had been seen only once since Picasso's death more than three years before. There was tittle-tattle that strange goings-on – the widow in black re-enacting the funeral and burning candles to her dead husband while communicating with his departed spirit – were taking place in Vauvenargues on the eighth day of each month: the day Picasso had died.

The one heir apparent nobody heard about was the young Bernard. Paulo's youngest child by his second wife was in Paris, living an increasingly pleasure-seeking life. Seventeen years old now, and with a taste for high living, Bernard had joined a circle of friends who lived for excitement. Drug-taking was customary among this circle. Someone who knew him at that time says that he took no interest in the squabbles going on between members of the family. He had no need to do so since his mother, Christine, was keeping watch on his behalf, and there was never any doubt about Bernard's place in the succession. With Paulo's death, he had become the sole legitimately born male heir.

In March 1976 both Bernard and his mother attended a meeting with the heirs (minus Jacqueline, who pleaded ill-health) at the Mas d'Artijyny at St-Paul-de-Vence. During the three-day meeting, Claude set out what he believed to be in store for them. They signed a legal agreement giving unanimous acceptance. Claude returned to Paris justly proud of his achievement. It now needed only Jacqueline's signature to make the agreement binding on them all and to put an end to the outpouring of money into the coffers of the financial and legal advisers.

In December of that year it really seemed that a settlement would soon be made. Claude's legal counsellors at last reached a compromise with his stepmother. Her agreement, he was told, was within sight. *The Times* in London went so far as to report: 'The Picasso heirs have reached agreement on a share-out.' Quoting Roland Dumas, the newspaper predicted that 'barring a spectacular last-minute upset, the inheritance will be distributed to the six heirs within six months to a year'.

At about the same time, a vital decision was reached regarding the process of selection. Once the *dation* was completed and accepted by the state, all works remaining would be placed in 'lots of similar value'. The six heirs would then, according to their allotted portion of the estate, draw for these. In declaring this Gaston Bouvenet, president of a court near Grasse, laid it down that the 'lucky dip' would be scrupulously conducted under the official eyes of administrator Zecri and his panel.

The year 1977 thus began in an atmosphere of hope and expectation for all concerned, even Jacqueline. She kept herself remote from material considerations, confining herself to keeping Picasso's memory alive. Nevertheless, she let Claude and the others believe that their goal was in sight and that she had no serious objection to their proposals for the settlement of the estate. She could always show her hand later. She was still in the old house on the hill where Picasso had died, managing the servants who came to dust and sweep out the silent rooms but seeing no visitors. Perhaps she feared that settlement would rob her of precious memories, forcing her to sacrifice so many of the beloved works under her care. That they, 'the others', had finally penetrated her defences and wriggled into possession of a large part of Picasso's estate must have been a bitter pill to swallow.

Already they were using it as their own. Claude in Paris had assumed control over Rheims' dossiers and photographs, setting up a 'Société Picasso' with offices in the rue de Lille. Paloma was talking grandly about 'her love' for her father, and her sadness at having been cut out of his life. Marina was twenty-six and living with a forty-year-old doctor in Paris. They had an illegitimate son, Gael, who was three months old. According to press reports she had already received a million-pound advance. In one newspaper interview she said she was 'afraid' of the approaching legacy. It did not 'really belong' to her, and she planned to put the Picasso millions 'to good use'. (Subsequently she put more than one of them into the restoration of La Californie, the beautiful Cannes villa she inherited.)

Many of these stories were exaggerated, but one or two underestimated the extent of the fortune and its implications for the heirs. They valued Picasso's whole estate at only £140 million when it was worth far more. Even after the *dation*, it came to £175 million. In London the *Daily Telegraph* boldly announced on 20 January 1977 what each of the heirs would get. For the first time, it said, it was possible to evaluate the exact division of the fabulous spoils. Where Claude had told the newspaper only three months before that 'for the moment our fortunes are just air, not gold ingots', they could now be reckoned in real terms. By the *Telegraph*'s estimate, Jacqueline would receive about £28 million: both Marina and Bernard would get some £36 million; Maya, Claude and Paloma would each receive in the region of £12 million – or one-third that of the 'legitimates'. This made £136 million in all, with 'the balance going to the state'.

But all this wealth depended on the market value of Picasso's art. Claude proposed that they should form themselves into a company to protect it. The heirs would agree never to sell their works without the consent of the others, and then only 'judiciously'. All proceeds from the substantial and increasing reproduction royalties, after paying the costs of the company which administered the permissions and fee collection, would be divided between them equally. The difficulty was that some of the heirs (Marina and Bernard especially) were in need of substantial amounts of cash for the upkeep of their inherited properties. Jacqueline was to retain Vauvenargues and the Mas Notre-Dame-de-Vie; Marina La Californie (but only after she had agreed to sacrifice some works of art for it). Bernard inherited Boisgeloup, which had previously been intended for his late father.

While Claude's suggestion would have helped to maintain the value of the works of all the heirs, the need to support their property and themselves came first. As Marina explains: 'We could not tie ourselves to that, though some people think we did. The real fact is that we are all free to do what we like with our works. If I wish, I can sell every one of my possessions and Claude can keep his. That is the truth. The only difference is with the reproduction rights, in which we all share equally. Otherwise we can do strictly as we like, sell or keep them.'

She has sold. In November 1981, Marina let Sotheby's in New York offer some of her grandfather's work. Contrary to popular belief the heirs can and do dispose of works. The art world knows this. It waits eagerly for each trickle of newly released works to come on to the market. Every dealer has hopes of securing them favourably, because the value of Picassos has increased since his death, and may well continue to increase. Experts believe that Picasso's later works, many of which were caught in the dispute over the estate, may yet rise considerably in value.

But the settlement still needed Jacqueline's agreement. In June, another distinguished legal representative, Maître Lefèvre, was reported to have obtained five signatures (to a further agreement) 'after two years of persuasion'. Later *The Times* in London predicted that 'barring spectacular last-minute upset, [the estate] should be distributed to the six heirs within six months'. It seemed that a major step forward had been achieved, that success was actually in sight. But then, towards the end of August, one of the shrewdest of Britain's Picasso-watchers in Paris, the *Standard* veteran columnist Sam White, reported that Jacqueline had reopened the case. As White said, it would be 'painful for everyone except the lawyers who might find themselves the chief beneficiaries'. Jacqueline, he wrote, was 'a proud, somewhat imperious woman' whose intransigence had been responsible for much of the haggling that had split the Picasso family. The lawyers were disputing the value she had put on Picasso's donation to the Louvre.

Sam White's keen ear had heard that Jacqueline was also upsetting the other heirs by refusing to give them access to Vauvenargues, Picasso's burial ground, and by refusing to submit to their demand for an option to buy it from her should she ever wish to sell. The widow, he said, regarded this provision 'as an insult'. To suggest that she would ever sell her husband's final resting place showed, in her view, 'lack of tact'. But Jacqueline was now gaining a measure of notoriety thanks to assiduous press coverage of her conduct towards her co-heirs. Less than a month after the setback over the option to purchase, shrinking from the spotlight of public attention, she signed her agreement to the terms of the settlement. Halfway through September 1977 the final papers were in the hands of Pierre Zecri, and *l'affaire Picasso* was, in the eyes of impartial observers, finally over. A pre-tax fortune of an estimated 1,251,673,200 French francs (or £144,702,104 at then current rates) was, after tax, to be cleanly and equitably distributed. The 'lawyers' picnic' was, everybody thought, at an end.

Then, in a final harrowing footnote to the whole sorry affair, came the news on 22 October 1977 that Marie-Thérèse Walter, Maya's mother, had hanged herself behind her garage door in Juan-les-Pins.

9

FAIR SHARES

The shock of Marie-Thérèse's suicide threw another shadow over the settlement, bringing yet more tragedy for the heirs to contend with. She chose the moment when everything was at last agreed between them, and her daughter Maya's legacy no longer in doubt. Jacqueline had signed a month beforehand. Maurice Rheims, working from photographs and his meticulous valuations, had contrived an ingenious way of dividing the spoils which seemed fair to all. Each of the heirs would draw lots for 'packages' of 'Picasso's Picassos'. While these would vary – some containing few but valuable works, others many more lesser ones – every package would be worth approximately the same amount. How many lots each heir would be entitled to draw would be determined by their legally fixed fractions of the inheritance. Thus Jacqueline drew the lion's share, Marina and Bernard an equal amount between them, and Maya, Claude and Paloma divided a further fraction. The lots were given numbers which, written on slips of paper, were drawn in rotation by all six who met to take part in Rheims' 'lucky dip'. Though chance played a part, it was agreed that this was the best way to avoid more bickering and dispute. In Claude's opinion, 'You can never get two members of the family to agree on anything.' Any other way of apportioning the vast hoard would no doubt have proved him right.

Fortunately for Marina and her guiding expert, Jan Krugier, a prior personal selection, in the region of one-tenth of each beneficiary's portion, was permitted. It gave the heirs an element of choice, an opportunity personally to pick out works which held sentimental value for them. The scheme also shrewdly guarded against possible later recrimination on the grounds that the works had been arbitrarily and unfeelingly assigned. Rheims, Pierre Zecri and others were greatly to be congratulated on finding such an equitable solution.

When the lots had been drawn and the properties apportioned – Jacqueline to retain the Mas Notre-Dame-de-Vie and Vauvenargues in her lifetime as well as a studio in Paris; Marina to have La Californie, which she would spend a part of her fortune to restore; Bernard to inherit Boisgeloup in Normandy – the settlement of costs took care almost entirely of what cash was left. Picasso's great wealth, the rolls of banknotes he had kept stuffed in drawers and jars against the fearful prospect of running out of money and returning to the poverty of his early life, had all but evaporated. Indeed, the bill for the 'lawyers' picnic' may well have exceeded the individual inheritance of each of the lesser heirs.

It is doubtful that Pablo Picasso had intended his bitter legacy to become such a costly joke. He can hardly have anticipated the scale of his professional cornucopia any more than he could have foreseen the tragedies that would ensue from his death, including the latest, Marie-Thérèse's suicide. Why she chose to take her own life when she did was understood by no one more than by her daughter. Maya had seen little of her mother latterly but she knew the power of the obsessional love she had borne for Picasso.

To Maya, her mother's decision came when the burden of
maintaining that rose-tinged illusion became too great for
an ageing woman alone. She was tired of commemorating
her love and wished only to join him.

A note from her mother left for her spoke of an 'irresistible
compulsion'. Maya understood this: 'You have to know
what his life had meant to her. It wasn't just his dying that
drove her to it. It was much, much more than that.' Maya
found letters from Picasso to her mother which told of a
love that burned like a naked flame. 'He told her many times
that she was the most wonderful, the prettiest, everything in
the whole world. But to be the most wonderful *grandmother*
in the world? She didn't want that.'

Two months before Picasso's death, Marie-Thérèse had
had a premonition of it. She confided in a letter to Maya:
'Something is very wrong. I fear for his life.' This anxiety
about her fitful lover was not uncommon. Maya knew that
her mother felt a compulsion to protect Picasso, however
far apart they were. 'Their relationship was crazy. She felt
she had to look after him – even when he was dead!
She couldn't bear the thought of him alone, his grave
surrounded by people who could not possibly give him what
she had given him.'

She seemed never to have wanted marriage with him.
When Olga, his first wife, died, Maya believes that Picasso
asked Marie-Thérèse to marry him and she refused. 'I heard
it from somebody working in my father's house, somebody
I knew well, and I am sure it was true. He rang my mother
and asked her to marry him. "Look," he told her, "Olga is
dead. We can be married."' Jacqueline, by then living
with Picasso, as Marie-Thérèse knew, was in his house;
Maya herself was in the next room, but Picasso never
bothered to conceal his most private emotions. According
to her daughter, Marie-Thérèse hesitated for only a few
seconds then told him: 'No, Pablo, it's too late now.' And
Picasso, dumbfounded, turned to the woman who later
recounted the story and cried: 'Can you believe it? She

doesn't want to marry me! Now that I'm at last free, she doesn't want me! Can you beat that?'

Marie-Thérèse's decision explains much of what was to follow. Maya says: 'My mother knew all about Jacqueline, and about Françoise and so on, because my father used to tell her everything in the long letters he wrote to her. She was under no illusions about my father. When she said no, she knew she was turning down the greatest love of her life, but she also knew she had to do it. It was, as she said, just too late.' Had she accepted, she would have shared his last years in Jacqueline's place. Perhaps it was too great a burden. She knew him too well, understood the tempestuous genie in him which sought change as keenly in love as in art. But if, as his widow, she had outlived him the disputes might have been less. She had seen his family driven apart, her daughter forced into legal battles. Now at last it was decided, all over. She had no more part to play, no more letters to write to her great love.

Picasso had not exaggerated when he predicted that the worst events of his life would be overshadowed by chaos after his death. He had made the prophecy a self-fulfilling one by deliberately leaving no will, sentencing his family to years of damaging squabbles, rancour and an enormous bill for the mechanism of obtaining a settlement. In life he had cruelly rejected his illegitimate children; upon his death even a recently revised law continued to discriminate against them. Yet they had emerged from the tangled web of the settlement negotiations as public, well-respected figures.

'The seemingly impossible is about to happen,' Claude told a reporter in April 1978, 'within weeks, Picasso's millions will be amicably divided among the six of us and the French state.' He talked wearily of the 'monumental muddle' left by his father, and of the clash of wills among the feuding heirs in courtrooms, and confrontations which had lasted close on five years since Picasso's death. What the newspaper called 'the most bizarre lucky dip in history' was over.

Had it damaged them all? Nothing could bring back Pablito to share in the bonanza of wealth. Or resuscitate Paulo and Marie-Thérèse. But Jacqueline, Claude, Paloma, Marina and Bernard were freed at last from the anxieties and disputes of the struggle.

Claude could afford a new motorcar, a Porsche, and many like it. He could talk openly of those years of anguished conflict. 'He has found a better way of living with his memories of a giant who cannot be judged by ordinary standards,' wrote London journalist Peter Lewis, who interviewed him in Paris at the time. But would he ever be able to forget the cruel hurt his 'giant' of a father had made him suffer? The reporter doubted it. 'His luminous dark-brown eyes, like his father's but less scorching, betrayed that the wounds had not healed.' Claude's devotion to his father's interests was, Lewis noted, 'remarkable, because of the treatment he received when Picasso met, and later married, Jacqueline Roque'.

Claude had grown up with Paloma in a top-floor studio by the Seine where Picasso painted *Guernica*: 'We had to live in three small attics.' He had been barred from seeing his father when he was fifteen. And, after Picasso died, he came back from America to the Château de Vauvenargues where the funeral was taking place to be barred again. 'I knew the telephone number but my stepmother would not take my call. She sent a message that my sister and I could not come to the funeral which was held inside the grounds. I could have got in. I knew where to climb. I knew the underground passages. But I didn't try. It wasn't the point, was it?' The point was that Claude had had to fight for everything he got. His mother had prepared the ground, and prepared it well, but his own strength and determination were instrumental in what he and the other *adulterins* accomplished.

And today Claude still cannot altogether hide the scars inflicted upon him by his upbringing and the struggle to obtain a part in the succession to his father's riches. At the opening of the Musée Picasso in September 1985 he paraded among the select privileged guests wearing a fixed smile. His nervous gestures, lined face and balding black hair were all legacies of the strain he has lived under. Already dogged by a worrying heart condition, Claude has had to live through a period of corrosive tension. His present work is partly with SPADEM, the French society for the protection of artists' rights, of which he is the valued president. His prestigious name and acquired knowledge of the art world – most especially the skulduggery whereby many publishers and unscrupulous dealers cheat artists and their estates of fees payable for reproduction of their work – lends SPADEM weight. He also administers the Picasso archives, sifting and sorting the works brought to him for provenance or rejection as fakes. His work is made all the more difficult as Picasso himself was known to have 'faked' canvases on occasion, signing a painting he knew was *not* by him in order that a poorer friend might sell it. To identify and catalogue any artist's *œuvre* is difficult. The task of keeping tabs on Picasso's phenomenal output requires every moment of the painstaking hours Claude devotes to it.

He seems happy and relaxed with his pretty American second wife, Sydney Russell, a palaeontologist, but the studied movements of his arms and legs lack co-ordination. She has a slight advantage in height, despite the low-heeled shoes she adopts, and her crowning beauty, a fine head of hair, seems to add to the impression of her husband's diminutive stature. Claude Picasso, who has his father's almost black eyes, is by no means insignificant, but one is surprised to find him so lacking in the strong, commanding presence which Picasso, despite his own short stature, had in abundance. Claude's first wife, Sara, was shocked by the change in him when they faced each other soon after Peter Lewis's Paris interview. 'Before we were married, Claude used to talk wildly in his better moods about what he'd do with the money when his father died. He was a lot of fun in those days. But in court he was the absolute opposite, a man without any spark of fun in his life at all.'

Claude's work is made no easier by a flood of queries from dealers and others seeking verification of works they believe to be Picassos, or claiming that Picasso in his lifetime had promised them this or that. The unexpected seriousness which so shocked Sara in New York has been born of this responsibility for deliberating between works which can be worth thousands, or nothing. When Claude signs an affirmative provenance confirming a work is by his father's hand it can change the owner's life. If he declines, the effect can be catastrophic. His Paris office, the headquarters of the Société Civile Picasso, is a retreat in which he can assume something of his father's mantle. He keeps voluminous ledgers, with coded references to each work of his father's set out neatly. These archives are the definitive record of Picasso's prodigious output, spanning nearly eighty years of artistic endeavour. Nobody denies that there may be fakes and forgeries among them, but every effort has been made to prevent this. In their most simplistic styles, unfortunately, Picasso's works are not hard to copy, and there will always be doubt over some of the works attributed to him, even by Claude. The fact that his father often left a work unsigned makes provenance doubly hard. But among dealers it is said that Claude has inherited his father's keen eye and has acquired considerable knowledge of the works.

Does the long struggle seem worth it to him? Claude says he had been 'reluctant at first to get involved'. But when he saw that Jacqueline was claiming everything for herself and Paulo, shutting out all Picasso's children born out of wedlock, the fight to establish his own and his sister's rights became a crusade. For a youngish man who did not originally want to get involved in the disputed succession he has shown remarkable maturity. He and Paloma have both had to develop new skills in dealing with the pressures of life in the public eye, a process which has changed them.

Where Claude radiates a newfound *gravitas*, a conscious-
ness of being the head of the family, Paloma remains carefree
and unaffected. If it's acting, it is good acting. 'I was
working,' she explains. 'And at the beginning I really didn't
want to do anything about it. But when I saw how things
were moving, with Jacqueline and so forth, I found I just
had to take part even though I kept on working, making a
film and so on, while I was doing so.'

She cares deeply about the effect of the inheritance on
her family without seeing very much of any of them. Eight
years ago, shortly before the settlement was finally made
and her father's fortune distributed, Paloma met and married the man who has since given her a second career,
playwright Rafael Lopez-Sanchez. The registry-office wed-
ding in May 1978 was a left-bank Paris spectacular. It was
followed by a banquet given by couturier Yves St-Laurent,
her dress was by the fashionable German designer, Karl
Lagerfeld, and the whole occasion was a public declaration
of her intention of moving into the upper reaches of international society. Paloma revels in the acclaim her work
receives. 'She appears to be the most successful of them all,
but it was very hard on her. It made her more outgoing,'
Françoise says. And marriage, it seems, was a firm step
towards self-fulfilment.

Paloma moves among the jet-set, frequenting fashionable
cities and the playgrounds of the Western world. She enjoys
the pace and the abrasive excitement of New York, much
as she once revelled in the adolescent street life of Paris.
She and her husband work together in theatrical ventures,
but chiefly she continues to expand in her own right. *Vogue*
has described her as 'the most exciting young woman in
Europe today' and it shows. The eponymous business she
has built up is rarely absent from magazines and journals
which chronicle the escapades of the glamorous and
wealthy.

She and Rafael are seldom seen in public with any of the
other members of her family, though she was with Claude

and Sydney in Paris for the opening of the Musée Picasso. Paloma spends most of her time in New York where she is busily decorating an apartment. She is cool, charming and amusing, giving no hint of the stress. So where are the scars she has had to share with Claude? 'I make sure they don't show.' She laughs. 'It's hard to know how badly hurt we all are because there was conflict anyway, even before this happened. In a way we only began to exist as a family afterwards. You know, I hadn't seen much of Maya, and Paulo I only said hallo to in the street now and then when we happened to meet. At least it did do that; we all suddenly became a family, which we never were before.'

She cannot make up her mind, though, whether 'the family' might have been happier to remain scattered without the battle over the inheritance to unite them. The paradox of her father's death bringing wealth and perhaps a closer unity to them all, while causing so much hurt and fatal damage, is a bitter one. 'It's hard to say if it is better that it happened as it did or not. But it is our life. It's not something we invented, or a charade. It is the truth. Even if everything tends to prove the opposite, there is no escaping the fact that we are our father's children and it was our fate to be that. We had to survive.'

For the other survivors, the impact of Picasso's disputed millions, his bitter legacy, has been similarly equivocal. Marina lives in Switzerland and the South of France, bringing up her children and putting her inheritance (three times as much as Paloma's and Claude's) to good use. A small, self-effacing woman of thirty-five, she suffered triple and terrible losses when her grandfather died, when the brother she adored committed suicide, and when her father, Paulo, succumbed to his alcoholism. At one time she seemed to have found happiness in Paris with a man she loved. They have two young children, Gael and his sister Flore. But the man, an anonymous doctor, is no longer her lover. A close friend hints at the reason for the break up of the relationship. 'He was a violent man, he treated her shamefully.' Marina herself will only say: 'It was a love story, a sad story, and it's over.'

So she is alone, apart from the children, the increasing numbers of stray dogs they find and bring back to her renovated villa, La Californie, in Cannes, and old friends. The house, where Picasso celebrated his new liaison with Jacqueline (and which an earlier mistress, Geneviève Laporte, found both 'enormous and over elaborate'), once belonged to the Moëts of champagne fame. There is little bubbling gaiety in Marina's life now. To have inherited some £33 million in works of art and property is one thing. But money, even Picasso's fortune, does not buy caring companionship. She would like to marry, to find another father for the children who have more toys than they know what to do with. It would be the ideal solution. 'Yes, I should like to make a new life, to have another child. One has to go on.' She must also try to wipe out the memory of recent tragedy.

Sitting quietly in her airy all-white drawing room, delicately relieved with splashes of daffodil yellow to match the curtains at the full-length windows, Marina talks candidly, seemingly strangely remote from the other Picassos. 'We are not a family,' she says simply. 'It's true that we are all scattered about, leading very different lives, but there is besides no feeling between us. I can't say today that I have a family.' In her view Jacqueline was never part of them. 'She lives in a separate world.' Marina was with her stepmother at the opening of the Musée Picasso in Paris, which was attended by the whole Picasso clan. Jacqueline, she says, moved constantly, as if trying to avoid any close contact with the others. 'She seems psychologically exhausted,' Marina comments. 'The strain has been too much.'

Marina's drawing room is dominated by one of Picasso's life-size canvases of Olga, his first wife, and by a magnificently stark Balthus painting, one of several works by other artists which she has bought since receiving her inheritance. Another is the fine Renoir in her sumptuous bedroom suite.

A staff of seven keep La Californie in perfect order. Two gardeners are at work on the magnificent lawned grounds. Panoramic views of the Mediterranean are obstructed only by the block of flats which so appalled Picasso in his lifetime, causing his removal to Mougins. The block occupies only a very small part of the vista, but Picasso saw it as aesthetic desecration.

When she tires of Cannes, or her children's schooling makes it necessary, Marina and her family return to their other home in Geneva where Jan Krugier, who gave her so much valuable help, has his gallery. They are still in touch. 'Krugier helped me to make a better choice. Some were not so lucky – Bernard, for instance. He had the same inheritance as mine, but my fortune is well managed.' She has, she claims, increased it three to five times. At the start I got about £30 million. Of course, it's relative: if the market is good, it can make all the difference. If it falls, or if you don't manage things properly, well. . . . Bernard can be poorer tomorrow and I can be richer, or the contrary. I think I have managed well.'

She has little to do with Claude and the Société Civile Picasso. 'He doesn't know what I do with my fortune. I act alone to run it. I'm not going to clash with him, but I don't do anything with him. I think I do quite well on my own.' Materially, she seems the most astute of the six. Jacqueline inherited as much as she did, but in Marina's opinion has made less use of her inheritance. 'She didn't have to pay so much in estate duties as us because she was Picasso's wife. We were his issue, and in France that means you have to pay more. So she *should* have ended up richer than us, but in the end she isn't. It's very complicated!'

Marina seems to have the strength of mind and independence to go her own way in handling what was left to her. Claude's concern, his reason for setting up the Société and the Picasso archives, was to protect the estate from forgeries and pirated reproductions, but he also tried to regulate the heirs' sale of their Picassos so that they would not deluge the market at any one time and bring prices down. This created the myth that none of the heirs was free to dispose of his or her inheritance without the consent of the others. In fact Marina has sold a number of works to help pay for the million-pound restoration of her beautiful Cannes villa, and to provide her mother with another lovely home nearby. It has led to criticism from the family, who question her need to liquidate so much of her inheritance. 'I don't know why she needs so much cash,' Paloma says. 'I think that somewhere in her mind she wants to get rid of all her Picassos. I mean, she's been through a lot. And maybe Father . . . well, she was never close to him. She was never raised to know what a Picasso painting might be. And I think that with Father dying, and what happened afterwards, she rather resents the whole thing. She is certainly selling with a vengeance!' Because she doesn't know what she wants, perhaps? Paloma thinks: 'She doesn't know what a Picasso is, anyway. She doesn't really want to know.'

In April 1980 an American tax shelter and art investment company was sued in the Civil Court in New York by the other heirs (with the exception of Jacqueline) to disclose the ownership of rights which Marina had agreed to sell for a reported $22.5 million. Martin Bressler, the New York attorney who handled the case for the heirs, claims he made a legal breakthrough in winning his case. Until then the whole issue of inheritors', or purchasers', rights to sell reproduction rights (in France, *droits morals*) had been a murky area. 'What we did here was something I'm really quite proud of,' Bressler says. 'We made a legal definition. Now, the Picasso heirs have the right to challenge each production and its use. If disputed, the individual case must go to Maurice Rheims as arbitrator. And from each reproduction fee paid, everybody gets something; all the heirs, Marina and Jacqueline as well.'

Since then profits from the reproduction of 'Picasso's Picassos' have been steadily mounting, increasing whenever world attention is drawn to one of the works. The firm which bought them, Jackie Fine Arts, can and does print them on to shopping bags, scarves, aprons and even jigsaws. The estimated annual revenue from reproduction rights worldwide is close to a million dollars. 'And we all share in equal parts. Everyone has the same,' Marina declares. At current rates, this probably means an income of approximately £100,000 a year from this legacy alone in every one of the six cases.

With that and their respective fortunes in pictures, mainly locked away in bank vaults, one would imagine that the long ordeal of the settlement could cheerfully be forgotten. Marina wonders if it is. 'From my point of view I can only say I am *not* happier. Not me, and I say that with no pretence. For the others? Well, Claude, Paloma and Maya have serious psychological problems, wouldn't you say? They have to bear my grandfather's name, and they have suffered a lot from that. In my opinion, now that they have all this money, they tend to believe that they have *become* Picasso. They live with that idea, which of course is totally untrue.'

Both Marina and her half-brother Bernard are multi-millionaires, which should make it possible for them to enjoy life as few in the world can. Marina doubts that, too. 'I believe Bernard and I, and my dead brother Pablito, suffered too much for happiness to come now. We do the best we can because it is our life and we can't refuse what it has brought us. It's no good trying to pretend that it didn't happen to us, because, after all, we have the name Picasso. But personally, for me, that is not happiness.' She prefers a simpler form of life, living for her children and the work of re-creating the splendour of La Californie, but she knows that she cannot have that alone. The burden of wealth, the responsibility it brings, must be shouldered.

She sold some of her seven thousand Picasso engravings at Sotheby's in New York in November 1981 to obtain money to buy other works of art, and to pay for the restoration and development of her property. She feels that the use of her inheritance in this way makes far more sense than keeping Picasso's brilliance locked away in the darkness of bank strongrooms. But it is not true to say that she does not care about her art fortune. 'I try to keep the best of what my grandfather left, and I have had everything restored.' She smiles a little sadly. 'You see, the inheritance does make life more complicated.'

In other ways, too, the heirs have paid heavily for their millions. Jacqueline, so far as the world can see into her shuttered life, is a tragic figure, devoting her existence to the perpetuation and glorification of her great husband's memory. With Paulo's death she lost her sole link with the scattered clans, and neither they nor anyone else except her daughter and a very few close friends visit her. If she has (which Marina doubts) become the wealthiest of the heirs, she has paid the biggest price.

They all seem marked by the conflict. Claude has lost the carefree air of his youth which Sara, his first wife, found so attractive. He appears to be weighed down by the responsibilities of guardianship, the never-ceasing duties of controlling his father's magnificent *œuvre*. Like the others, he now has to be conscious of the constant threat which haunts the super-rich, the menace of kidnap, trickery and theft. The works of Picasso are prized targets in the criminal underworld as gallery thefts have shown. Paloma's struggle for recognition in her own right is complicated by her wealth and position, making publicity a questionable avenue for her to use. In person she seems happy and assured, but the life she has chosen among the beautiful people demands not only riches but also youth. However strenuously she tries, only the former be conserved indefinitely. Marina, who lost so much, is perhaps the one most in need of support. She has delightful children and knows that they need a father. At present her properties and the pictures she buys and sells to increase the value of her inheritance provide activity and outlet. She must hope that the weight of her wealth does not come between her and eventual happiness.

Bernard, her half-brother, has been through bad times. His youthful activities in Paris, once it was known that he would become a multi-millionaire, were often injurious. Claude, it seems, has recently been guiding his nephew down safer paths, and the family feel that Bernard, now in his twenties, is ready to adopt a more worthwhile lifestyle. Paloma says: 'I hope, I hope, he is on the right road.' Marina and Maya wish him well. He lives mainly in Paris but has the old château of Boisgeloup to care for as well. His marriage to an Italian girl may also have helped to steady him. As he was the youngest, Bernard was the least affected by the struggle over the succession so we must wait to see how much or how little he makes of it.

Fortunately for Maya she has a full life which has insured her against any lasting ill-effects from the trauma of her mother's suicide. She has her lovely old apartment on the Seine in Paris, though her roots still seem to lie in Marseilles where she lived for years, and where her seafaring husband returns now and again on duty. Maya's robust sense of fun, her very Picasso-like love of mischief, gives the lie to any supposition of lasting sadness or permanent psychological damage. She, of all the heirs, seems as vital today as when she shared her father's life as a schoolgirl, listening in on his private world.

The storms and squalls of the succession have left six individuals with immense fortunes. The sale of only a few works by the master in today's market will produce for his heirs a sum far in excess of his entire lifetime's earnings. It is already clear that the heirs will not remain as rich as one another. But in every case they have been given not only the joy but also the drawbacks and problems of great wealth. The question they ask, and to which there is no answer except in the curious psyche of the man himself, is why Pablo Picasso left such a poisonous puzzle for them all.

10

THE FACE OF THE MINOTAUR

If there is a moral to the puzzle, it lies in the supposition that no man, not even one as wily and devious as Pablo Picasso, can play with fire without getting burnt. Picasso had trusted none of his children or grandchildren to safeguard his *œuvre* for posterity. He had, as Dumas said, 'left it to the law' and to chance. Ultimately, he abdicated responsibility, refusing to credit any of those destined to succeed him with sufficient acumen to ensure that his art, his genius, lived on. The result was that the collection was split up, distributed in job lots to each of the six, doubly decimated by the state's grab of a share. Hardly a notable success for the combined brains and expensive talents of seventeen professional advisers and counsels of the French legal system.

Maya is indifferent to many of her works, Claude obsessed by the need to catalogue and control their flow, Paloma escapes into mockery of the worst effects of the settlement, and Marina confesses herself unhappier as a result of it. Where is the torrent of joy which such an inheritance should have released?

Certainly not with the one who has been granted the lioness's share. Picasso's wealth has shed no golden light on his widow Jacqueline's life. Her inheritance is tremendous. It includes several works that Picasso personally gave her in his lifetime and which form a special untaxed addition (a *cadeau d'usage*) to her main inheritance. But what joy are they to her now? Jacqueline made one of her rare public appearances in the summer of 1985 at the Museum of Fine Art in Montreal, Canada. She was wearing a full-length black dress. Her wardrobe, it is said, lacks any other colour. The feet which had been taught to shuffle soundlessly whenever 'Monseigneur' was working moved listlessly in black sandals from picture to picture. She knew them already, since these were her 'Picasso's Picassos', her personal exhibition. She moves it around the world at her own whim with no reference to, or advice from, the official Musée Picasso in Paris.

Those who saw her in Canada said she made them think of a caged bird too quickly released from captivity or a domesticated animal frightened by freedom. It seemed that she could hardly wait to get back to the solitude of the old house in Mougins. She lives there alone now with less frequent visits from her thirty-year-old daughter, Catherine, who is said to be contemplating marriage after finding life in her stepfather's shrine of a home increasingly dispiriting. It is not surprising. Jacqueline does not answer letters. Her telephone number is more closely guarded than the pictures in her collection. Contact with outsiders – even as important as the President of France, François Mitterrand, who was with her at the select preview opening of the Musée Picasso in Paris in September 1985 – is kept to an absolute minimum. She does not like meeting people, certainly not strangers. She prefers to live as privately with her memories of Picasso as once she lived with the man himself. In her grieving mind it seems he does still live for her. Under his portraits of them both in Montreal she turned to face the press with the curious statement: 'Monsieur and Madame are ready to receive.'

Not for the first time Jacqueline made it apparent that she cannot accept that Picasso has left her. The American writer Deborah Trustman, who interviewed her in 1980 at home in Mougins, was greeted by Jacqueline on the telephone with the astonishing news that 'Mstislav Rostropovich and Galina Vishnevskaya were here yesterday, and Vishnevskaya sang all night *for me and for Pablo.*'

In person Jacqueline is diminutive, two inches shorter than Picasso. Her dark shoulder-length hair is turning grey. The eyes which Picasso painted jet black like his own in a succession of portraits are actually hazel, vague and distant. Trustman found Picasso's portraits of Jacqueline cruelly insulting. They were done in one of the last desperate bursts of energy he forced out of himself. Enjoyment of sex was gone, but the urge to possess and destroy women was still apparent in the savagery of these works. They are so anatomically explicit they lack eroticism. The only feeling they arouse in many observers is revulsion.

Yet they are a statement of his final opinion of women. It seems that his minotaur side was uppermost while he worked on these last canvases. For him 'goddesses' had ceased to exist. The 'doormats' were no longer the creatures of his dominant will. These portraits are expressions of his terrible contempt for the female sex, his loathing for its hold over men and a deep-rooted conviction of male superiority. It was as if the minotaur which had charmingly ornamented his earlier works – a potent, mischievous presence at the feasts of flesh – was balefully inside him now and forcing its way out.

Even Jacqueline accepts that women were not respected any more than children by her husband. 'Sometimes I dream that he loved me. Perhaps he did, perhaps he did not,' she told Deborah Trustman. It was an unusually humble and revealing confession from the woman who, in Sam White's words, is often 'imperious'. After her visit to the lonely Mas Notre-Dame-de-Vie, Trustman concluded: 'Perhaps Picasso used her up, drained her. Now all she has left is his image of her.' What is left is all there, Trustman says, in the 'destructive, brutal portraits'. She blames Jacqueline's dog-like devotion to Picasso for her present isolation. 'She's burned out,' she quotes a friend as saying. 'She had to adapt herself totally to his life. He would not permit her to be sick, or to show that she was tired.'

Certainly Jacqueline's appearance at the VIP preview of the Musée Picasso in Paris was for her an almost unique gesture. If she and Picasso were hermits together before his death, she has now retired almost completely into the seclusion of her two homes, spending long solitary hours in the rooms where he died. When she goes out it is usually to be driven in one of Picasso's cars (David Duncan believes Picasso may have left his beloved black Hispano and a white Lincoln convertible among others in the Mougins garage) to Vauvenargues, to visit her husband's grave.

According to Danielle Giraudy, curator of the Antibes Musée Picasso, 'She sets an extra place at the table when she has a guest.' It is for 'Monseigneur'. Thirteen years after her husband's death, Jacqueline still hesitates over the words, 'when he died'. 'Picasso and I were like this,' she told Trustman, intertwining her slender fingers. 'Sometimes I dream that I see him. Maybe I don't dream it. Maybe he was here.'

The shadow of the great man darkens her life. If Picasso had planned it, his final subjugation of this woman who became his physical and spiritual slave could not have been more complete. Jacqueline gave herself willingly, and he took all that she had to offer. 'His greatness was that he accepted the suffering of the pain he inflicted,' Françoise says. 'He was always ready to undergo the same torture he made others endure. In my mind that makes him a tragic figure. He had all the *gestalt*, the lust for power, et cetera, yet at the same time he was ready for punishment. That is why he said somewhere that he was a "Christian satyr". He had both the pagan strengths and the Christian acceptance of suffering.'

A minotaur with an angelic paintbrush? Françoise rejects the image. 'No, not that. It [the minotaur] is a reflection of his guilt. You know, he was hypersensitive about every hurtful thing he had done in his life but could not help himself doing. When he was about fourteen, when he knew that his father's eyesight was going, he would not paint him because he wanted to go in another direction. I know he felt guilty about that, about his father giving up altogether as a painter and giving Pablo all his tools and so on. It is not simple, but I just think that this guilt, about this and many other things, was the force inside him which made him ill at ease with his children. I think it stems from those early, formative years.'

The contradiction is that Picasso left on record his actions against his own children, and did everything he could to prevent them inheriting his fortune. The fact of his rejection of Maya, Claude and Paloma will not fade away with time, and nothing will ever excuse it. Yet he seemed unaware, this hypersensitive artist, of the distress he caused them. 'They never made any effort to talk to me,' he is reported to have told a lawyer friend. Can he have been so blind to the efforts they were making during the last twelve years of his life to gain access to his shuttered world? It is not easy for them now to divorce the image of a man who could make such seemingly heartfelt statements from that of Picasso the minotaur.

Paloma was too young to be deeply wounded by her mother's separation from Picasso, but Claude felt it keenly. He and Jacqueline were never close. During the early holiday visits in his teens he maintained an air of cordiality towards her, but it is clear from later statements of his that it was a pretence. 'Nevertheless, when the door slammed shut,' he told American writer Roland Gelatt, in an interview for the *Saturday Review* published on 12 November 1977, 'it was like a bolt of lightning.' In his young mind the reason for their rejection had to include Jacqueline. 'Maybe I could see a little too much of what was going on,' he told

Gelatt. 'That bothered my stepmother. She was always jealous of my sister and me. It troubled her, I guess, that we should be around to bring back memories of the past.'

A past in which Françoise, his mother, had given Picasso the children she, Jacqueline, was sadly unable to bear him. Had there been just one offspring from her marriage to Picasso it would have been enough to rob Claude and Paloma of their places within the privileged circle of succession. She had to turn to other means, first by espousing Paulo's cause and then by opposing the 'others' in law. No doubt she had watched her countrymen playing their native game of *boules* and seen how a player deals with the unwanted intrusion of an outsider, risking all in one throw to cannon it from its place of advantage. Claude, Paloma and Maya were too near the jack. Her excuse, her cannon-ball, was the book Françoise had written – the explicit *Life with Picasso* as Jacqueline had never lived it. Yet Claude told Gelatt: 'I really never knew why Paloma and I were suddenly no longer allowed to see him. I don't know if it was the book, or whether it was because he was "gaga". I wasn't allowed to see him after I was sixteen and a half to tell if he was gaga or not.'

Paloma shares Claude's disbelief. She doubts that her father ever read their mother's controversial book. But Deborah Trustman, writing in the *New York Times* magazine in April 1980, claimed that one of the lawyers argued the opposite. 'He feels it was Picasso who made the children choose between himself and their mother. "Of course he read it," the lawyer says. "It made him very angry, and he transferred the anger to the children!"' If that is true, then there would be far less reason for Françoise or anyone else to seek redress. A man wronged by his ex-mistress, a great artist publicly and wilfully betrayed by revelations of his private life, could hardly arouse bitterness by his rejection of their offspring, however abruptly and callously. Jacqueline's support for her husband, too, would be wholly excusable.

The dates tell a different story. Françoise's book first appeared before the public gaze in the winter of 1964 in America, and not until the following spring in France. Picasso's refusal to let her children continue their visits to him and his wife occurred, they insist, in the previous year. Yet Picasso seems to have been blind, or blinded, to these plain facts. Roland Dumas received a letter from him written during the 1971 court proceedings when the children were trying in vain to establish their rights of inheritance. 'It's not me who has taken my distance from Claude,' Picasso wrote. 'It's *he* who has left me. How can he have forgotten the affection I always lavished on him?'

Claude had by no means forgotten. His suicide bid spoke more loudly than words. According to both his mother and his sister he was lastingly damaged, however he may now wish to make light of the wounds, by his volatile father. His ex-wife Sara was shocked when he told her how, one day while staying at the Mas shortly before the ban on his holiday visits, Claude ventured into his father's studio while Picasso was painting and infuriated him by giving an honest opinion of the work in progress. 'His father asked what he thought, and Claude told me he just said something about it not being as good, or as likeable, as other paintings he had done. Picasso seized the painting, wet with fresh paint, and hit Claude over the head with it, he was so angry!'

Sara was surprised at the paucity and pettiness of some of Picasso's gifts to his son. 'There was one picture Claude showed me which Picasso had sent to him while he was in boarding school. It was just a poster, a one-dollar thing like you could pick up anywhere in New York art shops. Pablo had actually signed it "To my son, from Picasso" – as if it was a valuable work of art!' To her mind such thrift was inexcusable, even if Picasso rightly believed that entrusting any more valuable work to a schoolboy would be foolhardy. She believes Claude suffered from his father's meanness, with an insecurity about money he never wholly lost. Françoise noted it during their life together: 'He was always

needing reassurance – actual cash in hand. Nothing I could
tell him, such as the fact that he was so much beyond all
that and that everybody knew it except him, had any effect.
It was an inner anxiety which came from his early poverty,
and he never lost it. He could never be completely re-
assured.'

Claude told Sara his father had no idea of the value of
money. Once he handed his son two hundred dollars to buy
a pack of cigarettes, then was astonished to see all the other
goods Claude had managed to buy with the money. 'How
did you get so much for so little?' Picasso asked in genuine
surprise. Claude told Sara that trunks stuffed with bank
notes lay around in his father's various houses. They were
a family joke. A story they liked to laugh over – true –
concerned Picasso's crestfallen expression when someone,
probably Jacqueline, pointed out one day that many of
the piled-high bank notes were worthless, having been
superseded in French currency by newer bills. He could be
equally careless with works of art. During the long process
of evaluating the estate, Maurice Rheims was constantly
astonished by Picasso's idiosyncratic way of preserving even
his most treasured possessions. It is said that the great
French art expert nearly suffered an apoplectic fit when he
found an old toothbrush rolled up inside a canvas painted
by Picasso's great friend, Georges Braque.

In the thirty or so years since she left him, unable to
put up any longer with his insufferable waywardness and
dominating behaviour, Françoise Gilot Salk has thought
deeply about Picasso's character. She sees Marie-Thérèse's
suicide as falling within a typical pattern of reaction to him.
To her, those who loved Picasso seem too often to have
been fatally afflicted to ascribe the tragedies to chance. She
was in California when the news of his death reached her.
'It didn't seem all that important. One of the children must
have called me from Paris, I don't remember. It wasn't a
big event for me by then, only for them.'

But when Jacqueline showed her claws, demonstrating

unmistakable antipathy towards Claude and Paloma, barring them from their father's funeral and setting in train the events which so tragically resulted in Pablito's suicide, Françoise began to formulate certain theories about her ex-lover. One of these concerned Picasso's fear of finally succumbing to his fate; he shared the superstition common to many Spaniards that to think of death is to invite it. On the other hand he knew very well that he had to protect his legacy. The care he had taken to amass and build up the representative collection of his work, 'Picasso's Picassos' now in the Musée Picasso in Paris, shows how concerned he was that his *œuvre* should be fully understood and respected. He wanted his work to be taken care of by those who could recognize its true value. He also knew that the family would be at each other's throat over who should inherit which of this works, and that for the most part they did not know a great deal about art. Claude, Paloma and Maya were the only ones, he believed, who would fully appreciate the artistic value of his legacy. The others would be anxious to acquire their portion for monetary gain alone.

Well ahead of time, Picasso had *planned*, let alone known, that there would be dissension and difficulty in his succession. Françoise believes he took pleasure in the prospect. 'It was left to Claude, who was really an angel, to be the faithful son to a very unfaithful father. Claude had to try to bring all the heirs together, to persuade them what must be done to benefit not only them but also his father's reputation. There was no easy way to do this because each had his own ideas.'

Those like David Douglas Duncan, the veteran American photographer who guards his intimate connection with Picasso and Jacqueline with the delicacy of a tightrope walker, can see no harm in Picasso's having shut his progeny out of his life. 'He adored his children,' Duncan says. 'He and Jacqueline lived very simply. Why, I've shared meals with them on the kitchen table and I'm absolutely sure he never meant to stand in the way of whatever rights they had.' If so, he had a strange way of showing it. Claude's own painting showed promise as a child. Paloma remembers him poking fun at his father, signing drawings he had done 'Henri Matisse' and telling Picasso, 'Now, there's a *real* painter.' When Picasso rose to the bait and asked how his son could say such a thing to him, Claude replied, 'Because his house is like his paintings – which yours aren't at all!'

If Picasso's paintings were joyful while his home life all too often reflected a growing dissatisfaction with his children, one must remember the telling words recorded by his mistress Geneviève Laporte in her book *Sunshine at Midnight*. 'I love what belongs to me, yet at the same time I have a strong urge to destroy,' Picasso told her. 'It's the same with love. Any desire I have for procreation is an expression of my other desire, namely to free myself from the woman in question. I know that the birth of a child will be the end of my love for her. . . .' Perhaps this explains some of the hurt he caused by his decision to die intestate, leaving all those he apparently loved, and who loved him, to fight and squabble over his immense fortune. The wounds of these battles will become invisible with time, but the memory of them distorts his image. There is a massive contradiction in the nature of a man who could paint *Guernica*, an expression of horror at man's inhumanity to man, the bombing of a defenceless city, and yet leave so many casualties among his own kith and kin.

Pablito's suicide may have been due to emotional instability and impetuosity of a sort nobody could have forecast, but his anguish and its cause cannot lightly be dismissed. He was driven to suicide, his sister Marina makes plain, by what had gone before. 'When he tried to see his grandfather the previous time, that day in August 1972, Jacqueline had him thrown out. She sent her secretary after him and unloosed the dogs. He had his identity card to show who he was, but still they treated him like that, calling the police and throwing his motorcycle in the ditch.'

Afterwards, Marina says, Jacqueline blamed Pablito's

parents for letting their son try to force himself on his grandfather 'when Picasso was busy working'. 'She always made my parents responsible although they were not responsible parents. My father was on very bad terms with my mother. He didn't work, he was idle, waiting every month for the money my grandfather sent him. He drank heavily. I think in his mind we were very far away from him.' Yet when he died Marina dutifully attended his funeral. Since she has inherited her fortune Marina has given her mother, Emilienne, everything she can possibly want. Her debt to these 'irresponsible parents' has been more than repaid. It is a debt which might never have been incurred had Picasso not turned against his son's first wife and family; if, perhaps, Paulo had been brought up by his father to inflict less pain and suffering on those close to him.

When his illegitimate children were born, Picasso signed their birth certificates 'father unknown'. In his eyes he showed more than enough generosity later, by giving them the right to his famous name. How they felt about his banning them from all contact with him once they were no longer amusingly young and pretty to paint seems not to have concerned him. Perhaps it never occurred to him also that his descendants could be crushed by the sheer weight of his indifference while, ironically, they would have to fight, expensively and bitterly, to establish their legal and moral right to the Picasso legacy after his death.

The name of Picasso certainly carries a damaging potency in its syllables. Pablo Picasso, the great humanist, the man who bred doves on the beautiful veranda of La Californie – painting them in supplication for peace – was the architect of a succession which has been more mischievous than any caprice of a 'Christian satyr'. This surely is the minotaur, laughing all the way down to his cloven hoofs.

AFTERWORD

Jacqueline Picasso's death on 15 October 1986 opens another chapter in the bitter legacy of Picasso's disputed millions. Who will now inherit her great wealth?

It also leaves unanswered the question she would never face: what justification had she for shutting Picasso's children and grandchildren out of his life?

Jacqueline paid no death duties on her inheritance under a 'contract of marriage'. The family believe that now half will go, after duty, to her daughter by her previous marriage, Catherine Hutin, and half to the Musée Picasso.

Jacqueline's suicide perhaps gives one clue to her strange purpose. She lived only for Picasso, and she wanted no one to share his genius. In the end, the burden of possession became too great to bear.

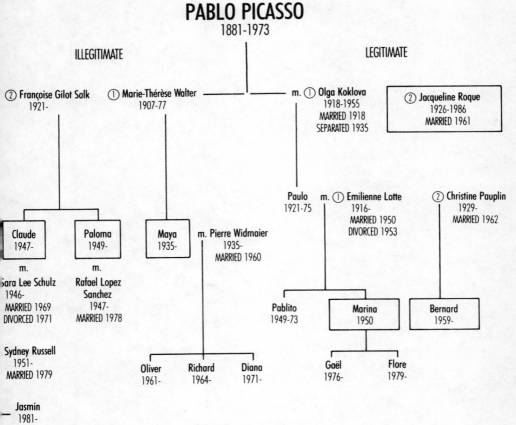

PABLO PICASSO
1881-1973

ILLEGITIMATE

LEGITIMATE

② Françoise Gilot Salk
1921-

① Marie-Thérèse Walter
1907-77

m. ① Olga Koklova
1918-1955
MARRIED 1918
SEPARATED 1935

② Jacqueline Roque
1926-1986
MARRIED 1961

Paulo
1921-75

m. ① Emilienne Lotte
1916-
MARRIED 1950
DIVORCED 1953

② Christine Pauplin
1929-
MARRIED 1962

Claude
1947-

Paloma
1949-

Maya
1935-

m. Pierre Widmaier
1935-
MARRIED 1960

m.
Sara Lee Schulz
1946-
MARRIED 1969
DIVORCED 1971

m.
Rafael Lopez
Sanchez
1947-
MARRIED 1978

Pablito
1949-73

Marina
1950

Bernard
1959-

Sydney Russell
1951-
MARRIED 1979

Oliver
1961-

Richard
1964-

Diana
1971-

Gaël
1976-

Flore
1979-

Jasmin
1981-

THE PICASSO CLANS
LEGITIMATE AND ILLEGITIMATE
(THE SIX HEIRS ARE FRAMED)

INDEX